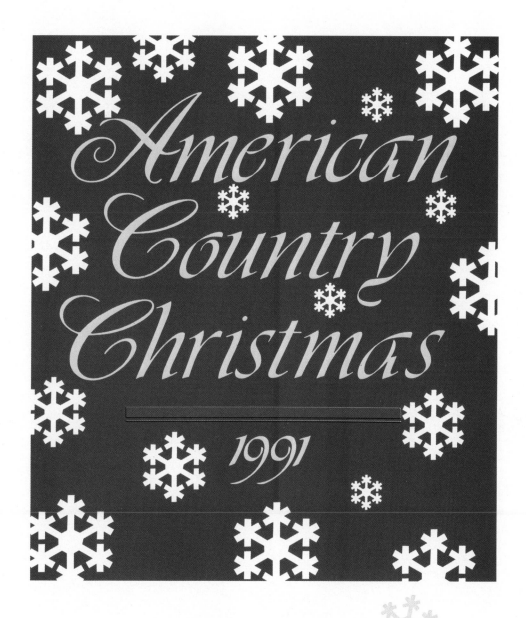

American Country Christmas

1991

COMPILED & EDITED BY
PATRICIA DREAME WILSON

Oxmoor House®

©1991 by Oxmoor House, Inc.
Book Division of Southern Progress Corporation
P.O. Box 2463, Birmingham, Alabama 35201

Library of Congress Catalog Number: 89-61909
ISBN: 0-8487-1051-7
ISSN: 1044-4904
Manufactured in the United States of America
First Printing

Executive Editor: Nancy J. Fitzpatrick
Director of Manufacturing: Jerry Higdon
Art Director: Bob Nance
Copy Chief: Mary Jean Haddin

American Country Christmas 1991

Editor: Patricia Dreame Wilson
Assistant Editors: Karen Broun Brookshaw,
    Heidi Tyline King
Contributing Editor: Charlotte Hagood
Editorial Assistant: Lelia Gray Neil
Designer: Melissa Jones Clark
Assistant Copy Editor: Susan Smith Cheatham
Senior Photographer: John O'Hagan
Photostylist: Katie Stoddard
Artists: Barbara Ball, Larry Hunter
Production Manager: Rick Litton
Associate Production Manager: Theresa L. Beste
Production Assistant: Pam Beasley Bullock
Recipe Development: Elizabeth Taliaferro
Test Kitchen Home Economist: Jan A. Smith

Contents

In my kitchen hangs a picture of a Christmas stocking. Emma, a nine-year-old friend, drew it for me. She did a beautiful job. The shiny silver stocking is decorated with a yellow lion, a pale green lamb, and the bright blue earth.

Every morning, I step into the sunny breakfast room to find this hint of holiday sparkle hanging in the air. I hope *American Country Christmas* gives you that same kind of pleasant surprise all year-round. In these pages you'll find many different ways to rediscover and re-create the childlike magic and simplicity of the season.

When I think of the Christmas spirit, I think back to the drawing in my kitchen. The cuff of the stocking reads "Peace on Earth." That's the best Christmas wish of all.

Patricia D. Wilson

Country Christmas at Home

Decorating with Nature's Bounty

In colonial times, fresh flowers and herbs, bountiful in summertime, were dried and fashioned into wreaths and arrangements. These refreshing decorations were then taken inside as reminders of summer during the bleaker fall and winter months. Today, holiday wreaths and dried arrangements are as popular as ever, perhaps for the same reason, and can be made from any natural materials that are suitable for drying. (For information on how to order dried materials, see the source listing on page 154.)

Wreaths of Welcome

The two wreaths showcased here are based on the foliage of dusty miller and lamb's ear, but other leafy plants, such as lavender, horehound, santolina sage, and thyme, will work as a base material. For drying, purchase or gather twice as much fresh base material as you think you'll need, since drying causes shrinkage. Lay the material on newspaper to dry for two to three days or until it is pliable and has the feel of leather.

To make a wreath, begin by wrapping twine around a purchased straw wreath form, with wraps 1½ inches apart. Tie florists' wire around the top of the wreath to form a hanger loop.

Cover the wreath form with base material by pushing the stem end of the base material under the twine to secure it. Wire together smaller branches and leaves in bunches with florists' wire before inserting into the wreath. For best coverage, place the material alternately on top of the wreath form and at the sides. Work so that the top of one branch overlaps the base of the previous branch and points in the same direction.

When the base of the wreath is fully covered, add clusters of dried flowers or seasonal decorations as desired. To protect the wreath and to reduce shedding, spray it with hair spray.

Above: Accents of pink and peach strawflowers and red and white globe amaranth are tucked into dusty miller and hot-glued into place. Small red glass balls on florists' picks add Christmas sparkle but can be removed after the holidays to give this wreath year-round appeal.

Left: Lamb's ear and tufts of Silver King artemisia are intermixed to create a complementary flow of green and silver hues. Dried roses encircle the wreath, while clusters of small red glass balls add a lively touch of color. When choosing flowers to dry, keep in mind that colors will change as they dry. (The light pink roses used here have dried with highlights of mauve.) After cutting fresh roses, place them in water and allow the buds to open slightly. Then clip the stems close to the bud and let dry for several days on newspaper.

Tabletop Topiaries

Another natural approach to holiday settings, table-top topiaries are fresh alternatives to wreaths and can be made with fewer natural materials. Referring to instructions for wreaths, purchase or gather fresh materials, tying into bundles if needed for fuller coverage, but do not allow to dry. Strawflowers, horehound, dusty miller, rosemary, globe amaranth, and cockscomb were used for the five topiaries shown here. German statice could also be used.

When the topiary ball is finished, it will be almost twice the size of the ball used as its base, so choose a 1½-inch to 2½-inch craft foam ball for a small topiary and a 3-inch ball for a large topiary. With a pencil, poke holes ¾ inch to 1 inch apart around the ball in a diamond pattern.

For the trunk, cut a thin branch, preferably one entwined with a vine or covered with interesting bark, a little longer than the desired finished length. Stick one end of the twig halfway into the bottom of the ball.

Attach the natural materials to the foam ball by filling the pencil holes in the ball with low temperature hot-glue and then pushing the stems into the holes. After the materials start to dry in a day or two, use any remaining natural material to fill in gaps.

Position the topiary in a container filled with aquarium gravel and topped with sheet moss. (Use florists' clay in addition to aquarium gravel to position large topiaries.)

Below: In this elegant arrangement, topiaries in dainty teacups surround a larger topiary. The two trees on the far left are made of strawflowers and horehound. The dusty miller topiary in the center sits atop a thin branch spiraled with a vine that gives the effect of a braided tree trunk. The tree to the right of the center topiary has a top of rosemary with globe amaranth tucked around it, while the one on the far right is covered with cockscomb broken into sections.

Above: These cone-shaped topiary trees look as if they came straight from a wintry wonderland. The two larger trees are made from great mullein and tied at the top with cranberry-colored bows. The small lamb's ear tree is wreathed with dried roses and ribbon streamers.

Cone-Shaped Topiary Trees

In addition to the traditional topiaries, cone-shaped topiary trees can be a striking way to bring the outdoors inside.

Referring to the instructions for wreaths, purchase or gather fresh materials and let dry. Working on a craft foam cone of the desired size (use a green cone if the materials dry green), begin at the bottom and attach a row of dried materials with florists' pins or hair pins around the base of the cone, allowing materials to drape below the bottom edge of the cone as shown in the photograph. Continue attaching materials to the cone, working in rows toward

Right: Balls of globe amaranth and Victorian cornucopias filled with a variety of dried materials make this a true garden garland. Make the pink globe amaranth ornaments in the same manner as the tabletop topiaries. Use straight pins to fasten a ribbon bow and hanger to each ball. The pattern for the cornucopia is on page 128. Cut the pattern from heavyweight decorative paper. To make a three-sided cone, fold along the fold lines and glue the flap to the inside of the opposite edge with craft glue. Secure the top side edge with a staple. Glue the end of a ribbon to each side for a hanger and embellish the cornucopia with scraps of ribbon or other trims.

the top of the cone and overlapping the ends of the materials for better coverage.

To cover the top of the cone, tie the ends of the dried materials together with a ribbon. For a crowning finish, add ribbon bows or hot-glue clusters of flowers around the cone.

Shades of Lavender

Imagine the wonderful scent and color contrast when you decorate your tree with lavender and Mexican sage. These fragrant wreaths and balls are easy to fashion and will make delightful natural ornaments or special gifts to use like sachets.

For each wreath, form a five-inch circle with heavy-gauge florists' wire and wrap extra wire around the circle twice. Work fresh flowering Mexican sage

spikes gently around the wire, tucking ends between the wires to secure. Use as many spikes as needed to make a full wreath. For added security, tie ends of spikes to wreath with matching thread.

When the wreath is completely dry, spray it with hair spray to reduce shedding and to protect it from humidity. Hot-glue a bow to the bottom of the wreath.

For the lavender ornament, stick a pencil into a 2½-inch craft foam ball to use as a handle. Coat the foam ball with a thick coat of craft glue and then roll the ball in loose lavender, gently pressing down on the ball until the lavender sticks. Repeat until ball is completely covered. Remove pencil.

Referring to photograph, circle the lavender-covered ball with ribbons and glue in place, covering the pencil hole. Secure a ribbon bow at the bottom with straight pins.

A Houston Hideaway

Step into this log cabin guest home. Smell the fresh pine. Curl up on a cozy buffalo-plaid-covered chair. Prop up your feet on the rough willow coffee table and warm to the crackling fire. Looking around at the collection of skis and snowshoes that hang on the rustic log walls, a guest may feel as if she has just settled in for a holiday in the Adirondack Mountains.

Guests immediately feel transported. They feel as if there should be snow outside and a cold north wind in the air, say the owners of this cabin in Texas.

With eight children (who all live out-of-state) and their families to entertain regularly, this busy couple decided to build a guest cabin getaway right next to

Above: Luminarias light a way of welcome from the main house to the guest cabin.

Right: Bold buffalo plaid fabric, geometric Indian-style rugs, and white ceilings offer bright contrast to dark log walls. The Christmas tree is studded with wooden moose-motif ornaments collected in the Northeast.

8

their house. Settling on the decor was no problem. These transplanted New Englanders wanted their love for the Adirondack region to shine. They worked with interior designer Lynne T. Jones to create the authentic Northeast look. "My clients wanted the cabin to feel as if a mountain man could walk in any minute, carrying his snowshoes," Lynne says.

The couple collected many items on visits to Maine and New York—sleigh bells, a black bear lamp, and a Camp Adirondack sign for the front porch. Lynne came across antlers while scouring a taxidermy shop for rugged country accents.

"We worked on decorating the cabin in the summer," Lynne says. "Houston, of course, is very, very hot, but it seemed as if there should be a fire in the fireplace at all times. It's so convincingly a mountain cabin."

With numerous grandchildren to entertain during the holidays, the owners stock the cabin with plenty of games, books, and toys. They willingly share their bear collection, including a bright red wool fellow that usually sits in a child-size twig chair.

This Houston cabin offers guests a retreat from the grand scale of Texas to a small corner of the north woods.

Above: In this woodland scene, deer, bunnies, and a family of black bears come together in a mossy peaceable kingdom. The red wool bear is made by Pendleton.

Left: Why is this bear smiling? Because he's a fabulous fake! Interior designer Lynne T. Jones found the artificial bruin in a department store display and purchased him for her clients' collection. The copper Indian once spun in the breeze as a weather vane.

Below: Bright wool blankets rest at the foot of twin twig beds. Eye-catching rugs from New Mexico warm the wood floors.

Noel Door Banner

Proclaim your Christmas spirit with this appliquéd Noel door banner.

Materials:
patterns on page 130
tracing paper
water-soluble marker
¼ yard (45"-wide) red cotton
scrap of green cotton
1 yard (45"-wide) unbleached muslin
thin quilt batting
threads to match fabrics
red quilting thread
2¼ yards (½"-wide) red double-fold bias tape
1¾ yards (1½"-wide) plaid grosgrain ribbon
2"-diameter brass jingle bell
small eyelet screw
10" (½"-diameter) wooden dowel

Note: Patterns include ¼" seam allowances.

Enlarge patterns. Using tracing paper and water-soluble marker, transfer patterns and markings to fabrics and cut out.

For banner, cut 2 (10½" x 30") pieces from muslin and 1 piece from thin quilt batting. Mark each piece along long edges, 4" from 1 end. For point at bottom of banner, fold each piece in half lengthwise and cut a straight line from mark on sides to fold line at end.

Referring to photograph, center letters on 1 muslin piece, overlapping where indicated on pattern. Turn seam allowances under ¼", clipping as necessary, and hand-baste letters to muslin. Using red thread, hand-appliqué letters to muslin.

Using matching threads and following photograph for placement, hand-appliqué holly leaves and then berries to center bottom of banner in same manner as letters.

Stack muslin backing, batting, and banner top, right side up. Baste. Using red quilting thread, outline-quilt ¼" from edge around letters and leaf/berry motif.

Using red bias tape, bind raw edges of banner, easing excess bias tape at corners.

Make a double bow from grosgrain ribbon and tack to point at bottom of banner. Notch ends of ribbon. Run small piece of ribbon through hanger loop of bell and tack to bottom of bow.

To hang banner, cut a 2" x 10" piece of muslin for casing. Turn all raw edges under ¼" and press. Slipstitch long edges to top of banner back, leaving sides and ½" in top center of casing open. Insert eyelet screw into center of dowel and slip dowel into casing. Pull eyelet screw through seam opening to top of casing.

Above: The Dilworthtown Country Store sells bundles of fresh boxwood, rose hips, pinecones, and other holiday decorating materials. On the porch behind her shop and house, Audrey makes wreaths and stores baskets of dried natural materials.

The Dilworthtown Country Store

The rolling hills of the Brandywine Valley region have changed little in the 214 years since the British battled the American Revolutionary army on the banks of Brandywine Creek in 1777. Even now, country crossroads are little more than pathways.

At one such back-road intersection in the southeast Pennsylvania countryside stands the Dilworthtown Country Store. A makeshift hospital during the Revolutionary War, this landmark mercantile store is believed to have been in operation nearly 20 years *before* the Battle of Brandywine.

The sound of gravel crunching under automobile tires is the last 20th-century intrusion for visitors to Audrey and Doug Julian's store. A step up onto the long stone porch gives shoppers a sample of times gone by: split-oak baskets filled with fresh-cut box-wood and bright red-orange wreaths of wild rose hips stacked on long worn benches.

Inside, however, the assortment of items is not

Above: The village of Dilworthtown was once an important coach stop. Now the store is a National Historic Site, welcoming travelers from all states.

representative of a certain time but is Audrey's personal interpretation of formal country style. Handwoven wool rag rugs, pewter plates, and antique and fine reproduction furniture fill the interior. Old oak counters and display cases are the backdrop for colonial lighting and upholstered wing chairs. Bundles of dried flowers from Audrey's garden are interspersed throughout the collectibles.

These collectibles often find their way from the store into Audrey's home—just a step behind the counter. The door to the living quarters of the historic building opens to the same white-washed stone walls, dark-beamed ceilings, and deep-silled windows.

A feeling of comfort takes hold once inside the

Above: An old turquoise hutch warms in the slant winter sunlight of the Julians' back porch. The antique canvas-covered wire decoy is from North Carolina.

Julians' home. Worn wooden-plank floors, large old fireplaces, and timeworn quilts all add to the relaxed atmosphere.

"When I'm decorating the house, I can just run into the shop for candles or a wreath," Audrey says. Of course, it works the other way as well. "I have boxes of antique toys and baskets stored in the attic. I can pull from them when I put together a display for the shop."

A Williamsburg gift and accessory shop, the Dilworthtown Country Store attracts shoppers looking for the colonial style. People stop by the shop after visits to Williamsburg—for holiday decorating inspiration and to see Audrey's personal spin on the old colonial style.

"One Christmas I decorated with lots of dried pomegranates. I put them in bowls with popcorn. I hung them in garlands. I put them in wreaths," says Audrey. This repetition of one item gives the eye a unified background for the vast collection that is the Dilworthtown Country Store.

Here—where country is a way of life as well as a way of style—workplace and dwelling combine in comforting unity. As Audrey puts it, "This historic building sets the theme for what we do."

13

Above: A print of a painting by Edward Hicks, a 19th-century American painter, sets the theme for this mantel decoration. Audrey furnished the old log cabin with her daughter's dollhouse furniture.

Left: Audrey brings out her red and white quilts for Christmas, but she's quick to point out that she would never really serve a meal on her friendship quilt. The ornaments on the Fraser fir are a collection of handmade tin, wood, and paper, mixed with German blown-glass shapes.

Above: Audrey is actually a very selective collector. "I only collect enough of one thing to fill one compact area," she says. Here, her entire Santa collection stretches across the divider between the kitchen and the family room. Each Santa is an original, made by artists such as Nancy Thomas of Yorktown, Virginia, and Judie Tasch of Austin, Texas. The snow under the Santas is batting from a worn-out quilt.

15

Above: Ron and Rhonda Erwin spent five years restoring an 1850s farmhouse and its one-acre grounds in historic Madison, Georgia. Ron finished most of the interior, while Rhonda restored the gardens to 19th-century authenticity.

A Victorian Christmas at the Boat House

Above: Some of the Erwins' antique dolls go for a holiday ride in a wicker sleigh. The red and green of the stained glass, which came from a church in England, enhances the Christmas decor in this music parlor.

Any day spent at the Boat House, a luxurious Victorian bed-and-breakfast in Madison, Georgia, is always special. But at Christmastime, this restored farmhouse takes on even greater charm.

Owners Ron and Rhonda Erwin begin early in the season to use their distinctive artistic touches to transform the almost 150-year-old home into a Christmas wonderland. The work comes naturally to the Erwins. By profession, Ron is an accomplished restorer of historic property, and both Ron and Rhonda are interior designers.

During the Christmas season, the fine Victorian furniture collections in every room at the Boat House are enhanced by unique and tasteful holiday displays. For instance, the Erwins decorate three 10- to 12-foot cedar and Georgia white pine trees inside the house with their collections of antique ornaments. A fourth tree, a 10-foot Georgia white pine, is placed on the comfortable wicker-filled front porch. Rhonda adds edible treats for the birds that nest in the many trees in the area.

The mantels on all 10 fireplaces, and many unexpected nooks and corners, are decorated with the Erwins' exquisite collections of antique dolls, doll carriages, angels, and pottery. The effect is that of a fairyland, where you wish you could remain forever.

Several years ago, the Erwins were captivated by antebellum Madison when they drove through the quiet little town on a trip to the North Georgia mountains. When they discovered the Boat House, which at the time was in great disrepair, including an unstable foundation, leaking roof, and leaning walls, they became enthralled with purchasing and restoring the potential treasure. After all, such restoration artists as Ron and Rhonda could not pass up what they felt would (and did) become a labor of love.

Not long into the restoration, the Boat House was added to three annual tours of homes—including the Christmas tour—because so many people wanted to see the work in progress. After five years of hard work and with an extensive collection of antique furniture in place, Ron and Rhonda knew that they wanted to share the Boat House with others. They decided to open up their home as a Victorian-style bed-and-breakfast.

The Boat House acquired its name when its first owner, Nelson Dexter, a sea captain from Rhode Island, built the house in 1850. Because of his love for the sea, Captain Dexter built the original two-room structure, now the formal dining and breakfast rooms, to resemble a ship's prow.

In another historical note, the Boat House was

Right and below: Late afternoon winter sunlight casts interesting shadows on the Boat House. On the front porch, the Christmas tree is adorned with cranberries and peanut butter-filled pinecones as a feast for birds. (These treats are quickly devoured by the birds and must be replaced several times each season.) Abandoned birds nests, baby's breath, and magnolia leaves complete the natural decorations.

Above: This glazed papier mâché 12-inch cherub trails a lace garland across a 10-foot cedar tree. Tiny colored lights, glass balls, and paper and silk flowers provide the perfect background.

purchased in 1866 by the Axson family. The Axson's daughter, Ellen, was President Woodrow Wilson's first wife. (Members of the Axson family are buried in the cemetery behind the house.)

The grand preparations for Christmas at the Boat House begin with finding and cutting four trees at a nearby tree farm. "When we go to cut our trees," says Rhonda, "it takes an entire day. After all, each one has to be perfect."

Above: Frilly pink bows, frosted blown-glass balls, and century-old dolls adorn this Georgia white pine in the upstairs sunroom. The books and toys under the tree are also antiques.

Below: The Green Room is an example of the Victorian luxury offered guests at the Boat House bed-and-breakfast. The doll riding sedately in the carriage is wearing a dress made from a 1910 wedding dress, and the elaborately carved bed makes a fine seat for the doll primly attired in green velvet. For information on visiting the Boat House, see the source listing on page 154.

Above: The appeal of this holly leaf and berry tablerunner is its simple, yet classic, design.

Christmas Holly with Accents of Gold

Dress your holiday table with the old-fashioned charm of this handsome holly leaf and berry runner. Use acrylic paints to stencil the leaf, berry, and border designs. Add details with outline stitching, couching, and French knots for an interesting textural effect.

Materials:
pattern and color key on page 129
tracing paper
18" x 50" piece of cream linen fabric
acrylic paints: green, red, gold
textile medium
small paintbrushes
embroidery floss (see color key)
embroidery needle

Using tracing paper, transfer stencil pattern to each end of linen, centering pattern and placing bottom of middle scallop 3" from end of fabric.

To stencil runner, follow manufacturer's instructions and mix textile medium with acrylic paints. Paint leaves green, berries red, and border detail gold. Let dry.

Place runner right side down on terry cloth towel.

Place a pressing cloth on wrong side of fabric and heat-set painted area, using a dry iron on warm setting.

Referring to pattern and using 3 strands of floss, outline-stitch all details except couching-stitch border. Work a French knot in each berry. For couching-stitch border, lay 12 strands of dark topaz floss on pattern line as indicated and couchstitch with 3 strands of light topaz floss. Continue couching around outer border.

To make fringe, use matching thread to zigzag-stitch 2" from each end of runner. Pull threads to within ½" of zigzag stitching line.

To hem sides, fold edges under ½" and then ½" again along both long sides of runner. Slipstitch hem. Place runner right side down on terry cloth towel. Place pressing cloth on wrong side of fabric and press.

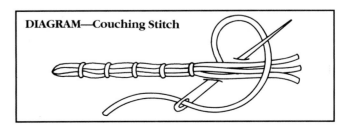

DIAGRAM—Couching Stitch

Old-Fashioned Quick Decorating

Paper projects are an inexpensive way to achieve a quaint country look for the holidays. Children will enjoy these projects that use the old snowflake and paper doll methods on folded paper to make dainty borders and festive table coverings.

Snowflake Table Covering

Besides the inexpensive materials, another advantage to this table covering is the clean-up. Once it has been used, it can be thrown away.

Fold a 41-inch square of brown paper in half diagonally three times. Referring to the Diagram, fold the short folded side to the long side. Trim excess at bottom where indicated. Enlarge the pattern on page 128 and transfer it to the folded paper. Cut out the scallop at the bottom, and punch holes where indicated. Cut out the remaining designs and unfold completely.

Above: A few scissor cuts and some hole punches transform folded paper into a detailed table covering.

Farmyard Fence

To surround a miniature tree, why not cut out this farmyard fence as an interesting alternative to the traditional tree skirt? Transfer the pattern on page 129 to the long edge of one sheet of white posterboard, starting and ending with one-inch overlapping ends and repeating the pattern until the fence is the desired length. Cut out the fence with a craft knife. Glue the overlapping ends together, holding them in place with paper clips until dry. For a freestanding fence, fold the fence accordion-style every five inches.

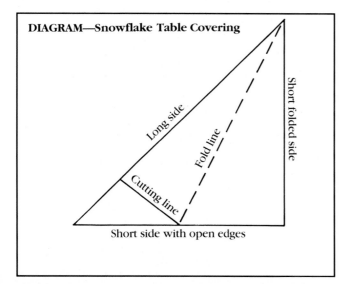

DIAGRAM—Snowflake Table Covering

Long side

Short folded side

Fold line

Cutting line

Short side with open edges

Country Borders

To make the newspaper border, tape ends of two single pages of newspaper together and fold in half widthwise four times so that the folded piece measures 2¾ x 14 inches. Transfer the heart pattern on page 130 so that it is on the fold line and the scallop is at the bottom of the newspaper. Cut out the heart and the scallop. Using a hole punch, punch holes where indicated. Unfold one fold of the newspaper and transfer the tree and the house pattern. Cut out and unfold completely.

To make the brown paper border, use an 11 x 40-inch piece of brown paper. Fold in half widthwise four times so that the folded piece measures 2½ x 11 inches. Transfer the heart pattern on page 131 so that it is on the fold line and peaks are at the bottom of the folded paper. Cut out. Unfold the paper one time and transfer the house and the snowman pattern. Cut out and unfold completely.

For longer borders, repeat the pattern two or more times and tape together.

Above: Evoke the feeling of an old-time Christmas by decorating the mantel with a brown paper border.

Above: The newspaper border serves as a delicate canopy for a willow bed. The border could also be used across a mantel or a doorway.

Left: Continue the farmyard theme by decorating your tabletop tree with animal cracker ornaments made by hot-gluing loops of ribbon to the cracker backs. Top the tree with a barnyard animal, such as this rooster, cut from a scrap of posterboard.

Holiday Handiwork

Whimsical Wonderland

What a treat it would be to awake Christmas morning and find your gifts waiting under this fancifully decorated tree! The country ornaments and *scherenschnitte* garlands are all lovingly handmade from primitive designs that evoke the feeling of the olden days. Multiples of the different decorations, which are made from inexpensive materials, are ideal family projects for a cozy weekend.

Twinkle, Twinkle

The shimmering icicles and twinkling stars that shine from the branches at left can be created in minutes by twisting glittery 12-inch chenille stems in various colors into the desired shapes. For each star, bend one stem in a zig-zag fashion at one-inch intervals, making a total of ten bends. Overlap the ends of the stem one inch to form a star. Twist the ends together securely; then gently mold into a pleasing star shape.

For each icicle, tightly coil one stem into a flat circle. Once the circle is formed, pull ends apart to form a spiral.

Snow Cowboy

Materials for 1 ornament:
patterns on page 132
tracing paper
4½" x 14" scrap of white wool
small amount of polyester stuffing
dowel for stuffing tool
water-soluble marker
size 5 pearl cotton: red, black
embroidery needle
11 small black-headed straight pins
4" x 6" scrap of black felt
threads to match fabrics
2 (3") twigs
½" x 8" scrap of red wool

Note: Reduce patterns by half to make small snowman on page 27.

To make snowman, with right sides facing, fold white wool in half. Using tracing paper, transfer snowman pattern and markings to top layer of wool. Using 12 or more stitches per inch, machine-stitch along outline through both layers, leaving open as indicated. Cut out snowman, leaving a ⅛" seam allowance. Clip curves and corners and turn.

Stuff snowman firmly, using dowel for hard-to-reach areas. Slipstitch opening closed.

Using water-soluble marker, transfer face and arm placement markings to snowman. Using red pearl cotton, embroider 3-wrap French knots for cheeks. Using black pearl cotton, embroider 1-wrap French knots for nose and smile. Insert 2 black pins for eyes and 3 pins in a cluster for each button.

To make hat, use tracing paper to transfer hat patterns to black felt and cut out. With raw edges aligned, stitch crown pieces together, leaving curved edges open. Trim seam allowances to ⅛". Clip corners and turn. Clip inner circle of brim as indicated on pattern. Slide crown through opening in brim, stretching opening if needed. Slipstitch brim to crown. Tack hat to head.

For hanger, cut a 7" length of black pearl cotton and fold in half to make a loop. Knot ends and tack to top back of hat. For arms, clip stitching between dots at each side seam and insert twigs. Fringe ends of red wool scrap and tie around snowman's neck.

Mosaic Mini-Quilt

Materials for 1 ornament:
scraps of assorted light and dark miniprint
threads to match fabrics
water-soluble marker
large-eyed needle
8" thin metallic cord

Note: All seam allowances are ¼". Finished size is 2" x 2½".

Cut the following from miniprint: 1 (1" x 10") strip each from 2 different light prints and 1 each from 2 different dark prints for pieced squares; 1 (2" x 2½") light or dark piece for backing; 2 (1" x 3") light or dark strips for side binding; and 2 (1" x 2½") light or dark strips for top and bottom binding.

To make pieced squares, with right sides facing and raw edges aligned, stitch 1 (1" x 10") light strip and 1 dark strip together along long edges. Press seam toward darker fabric. Repeat with remaining 1" x 10" light and dark strips. Following Diagram on page 26, place ruler at a 45° angle across strips. Using ruler as a guide, mark lines with water-soluble marker and cut across strips to form 1" squares, with each square consisting of 1 light and 1 dark triangle. Repeat to cut 12 light/dark squares.

To make quilt top, with right sides facing, raw edges aligned, and using photograph as a guide, stitch 4 squares into a vertical row, alternating squares as desired. Repeat to make 3 rows. With right sides facing and raw edges aligned, stitch rows together along long edges. Trim seam allowances.

To attach backing, with wrong sides facing and raw edges aligned, baste backing to quilt top.

Continued on next page.

To bind edges, with right sides facing and raw edges aligned, stitch side bindings to sides of quilt top. Fold to back of quilt, turn raw edges under ¼", and slipstitch in place. Repeat to bind top and bottom edges, turning ends under before slipstitching in place.

For hanger, thread large-eyed needle with metallic cord and stitch through top center of ornament. Knot ends to make a loop.

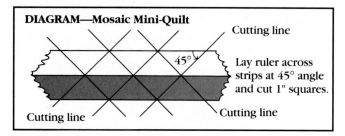

DIAGRAM—Mosaic Mini-Quilt

Cutting line

45°

Lay ruler across strips at 45° angle and cut 1" squares.

Cutting line

Cutting line

Cozy Christmas Cabin

Materials for 1 ornament:
pattern on page 132
tracing paper
1 (3" x 3¼") piece of 1"-thick craft foam
craft knife
red spray paint
jumbo craft stick
black permanent marker
hot-glue gun and glue sticks
garden pruner
¼"-thick twigs
1"-thick bundle of 6½"-long broom straw
red embroidery floss
embroidery needle
large paper clip
12" length (⅛"-wide) red ribbon
¼"-thick bundle of 8"-long green raffia
artificial red berries

Using tracing paper, transfer pattern to craft foam and cut out with craft knife.

Spray-paint foam cabin on all sides with red spray paint and allow to dry.

For door, cut a 1⅛" length from craft stick. Referring to photograph, mark hinges and doorknob with marker. Hot-glue door to center front of cabin.

Using garden pruner and referring to photograph, cut 3 twigs to fit on each side of door, with each extending ¼" beyond cabin edges. Cut twigs to fit cabin back, extending ¼" beyond edges. Cut twigs

for cabin sides, extending ¼" beyond edges. Hot-glue twigs on cabin front and back, spacing ¼" apart. Hot-glue twigs on sides, between those on front and back (see photograph).

To make roof, separate broom straw bundle into quarters. Using embroidery needle and all 6 strands of red floss, wrap floss several times around center of 1 quarter section of straw. Add another quarter section of straw and continue until all quarter sections of straw are wrapped together. Knot floss to secure and clip ends.

Repeat wrapping procedure 1" to left and 1" to right of center wrapping. Gently bend roof at center and hot-glue to cabin.

To make hanger, bend paper clip to form a U-shape and push through top center of roof and into foam so that only ¼" of paper clip is exposed. Pull ribbon through loop and knot ends.

To make wreath, twist raffia and shape into a wreath. Hot-glue to top of cabin front. Hot-glue red berries to center of wreath.

Mittens-and-Snowflake Garland

Materials:
patterns on page 132
2 yards (⅛"-wide) white ribbon with gold metallic edging
liquid ravel preventer
craft or parchment paper: light brown, cream
small sharp scissors
regular hole punch
⅛" heart-shaped hole punch

Note: For information on how to order special *scherenschnitte* scissors and supplies, see the source listing on page 154.

Cut ribbon in half. Apply liquid ravel preventer to ribbon ends and set aside to dry.

To make mitten pair, cut a 2" x 3½" rectangle from light brown craft paper. Fold the paper in half widthwise. Lightly trace mitten pattern onto paper, making sure thumb is on fold. Cut out along *solid lines only.* Gently erase any pencil lines. Using regular hole punch and referring to pattern, punch hole for ribbon placement. Unfold. Repeat to make 7 more mitten pairs.

To make snowflake, cut a 2¼" square from cream craft paper and fold in half. Lightly trace garland

Continued on page 28.

Rickrack Candy Canes

These candy canes look good enough to eat, but you'll find that they last much longer than their sugary-sweet cousins. To make five of these neat treats, cut one (40-inch) length each of ¾-inch-wide red and white rickrack trim. Tightly interlock the two lengths. Steam-press the rickrack on low heat as needed to keep it flat, since it has a tendency to curl as you interlock it. Cut five (eight-inch) lengths from the interlocked rickrack.

Cover a small area of your ironing board with waxed paper. Form the rickrack into five candy-cane shapes and pin to the waxed paper. Iron the canes to set the shape and let cool.

To stiffen the canes and to prevent raveling, first mix four parts of liquid fabric stiffener with one part water. With a small paintbrush, *lightly* brush the canes with this mixture. Let dry completely. Repeat the process on the other side of the canes. Trim the ends of the canes with scissors, rounding off the edges.

For a hanger, thread a needle with red pearl cotton and stitch through the top of each cane. Knot the ends of the thread together to make a loop.

snowflake pattern onto paper. Cut out along *solid lines only.* Gently erase any pencil lines. Using heart-shaped hole punch and referring to pattern for placement, punch heart holes in snowflake. Unfold. Press snowflakes with a moderately warm iron. Repeat to make 9 more snowflakes.

Thread 1 end of 1 piece of ribbon through 2 heart-shaped holes in snowflake and then through holes in 1 mitten set. Continue alternating snowflakes and mittens until you have strung 5 snowflakes and 4 mitten sets. Repeat with remaining ribbon and paper shapes. Tie 1 end of each garland together. Knot ribbon ends to secure.

Snowflake Ornament and Treetopper

Materials for 1 ornament or treetopper:
pattern on page 132
cream craft or parchment paper: 2 (4½")
    squares for 1 ornament, or 2 (8") squares for
    1 treetopper
small sharp scissors
cream thread
sewing machine needle for fine fabrics

Note: To make treetopper pattern, enlarge snowflake ornament pattern to twice its size.
Fold 1 piece of paper in half and lightly trace ornament or treetopper pattern onto paper. Using

scissors, cut out along *solid lines only.* Gently erase any pencil lines. Repeat to make second snowflake. Unfold. Press snowflakes with a warm iron.

Place first snowflake on top of second so that edges and holes are aligned. Using cream thread, medium stitch, and sewing machine needle for fine fabrics, machine-stitch snowflakes together down center, from 1 tip to the tip opposite it. Leave a 3" thread tail at end of 1 tip and knot ends to make a hanger. Knot threads at beginning of seam and clip close to snowflake. Open snowflake to make a 4-sided ornament or treetopper.

> ### *Scherenschnitte* Tips
>
> *Scherenschnitte* (sheir-en-SHNIT-ta) is a very old German craft that turns paper into finely detailed scenes or designs.
>
> The most important tool used in *scherenschnitte* is scissors. Scissors with short, sharp-pointed blades are perfect for the intricate patterns because they can cut finely and reach inner design areas. Embroidery, cuticle, and iris scissors work nicely.
>
> When cutting out patterns, it is best to begin with the center and inside features. This will give you more paper to grasp while cutting.
>
> To finish your projects, you can remove the creases by pressing with a moderately warm iron.

Reindeer at Night

You'll enjoy the simple stitching on this prancing reindeer, whether it is created as a charming gift for a small child or as a playful cross-stitched wall hanging for yourself.

Materials:
chart and color key on page 133
10¾" x 11⅝" piece of 28-count Nordic blue Jobelan fabric
embroidery floss (see color key)

Note: Finished design is 5⅝" x 4¾".

Using 2 strands of embroidery floss and stitching over 2 threads, center and work cross-stitch design on Jobelan cloth according to chart.

Using mild soap, wash completed piece carefully in cold water. Rinse thoroughly. Roll piece in a terry-cloth towel to remove excess water.

Place stitched side down on a dry terry-cloth towel. Press with a warm iron until dry. (Do not use steam.)

Frame as desired. (Finished project is shown in an 8⅛" x 8⅞" metal frame.)

A Boy and His Sled

This boy and his sled conjure up pleasant images of Christmas vacation—winter days full of snowball fights and sledding!

Materials:
patterns on page 134
graphite paper
1 (16" x 17") piece of ¾"-thick pine shelving
1 (20" x 22") piece of ¼"-thick pine shelving
band saw or jigsaw
sandpaper: 100 grit, 150 grit
wood glue
wood clamps
handsaw
1 (2") length of ¼"-wide wooden dowel
electric drill with ¼" and ⅛" bits
acrylic paints: red, green, blue, black, yellow, flesh, white
paintbrushes
fine-tipped black paint pen
satin varnish
1 yard of gold cord

Note: To reduce sanding, wipe away excess glue with damp rag as you work.

Using graphite paper, transfer patterns to wood as indicated. Cut out, using band saw or jigsaw. Cut 1 (4½" x 8½") piece of ¼"-thick pine shelving for top of sled. Beginning with 100-grit sandpaper and finishing with 150 grit, sand all edges of pattern pieces smooth.

Glue 1 sleeve to 1 arm. Reverse remaining sleeve and arm and glue together. Clamp each sleeve/arm piece together and allow to dry. Spread wood glue evenly over backs of sleeve/arm, hat/hair, boots, and coat/scarf pieces. Referring to pattern for placement, position pieces on each side of boy, secure with wood clamps, and allow to dry.

Using handsaw, cut dowel into 2 (1") lengths. Place boy on base over dowel hole placement marks to make sure holes are centered underneath boy's boots. Referring to patterns and using ¼" bit, drill ½"-deep holes in center of bottoms of boots and on base. Using ⅛" bit, drill hole through each hand. Glue dowels into bottom of boy's boots. Sand all edges smooth.

For sled, glue runners to sled top, 2" apart.

Paint boy, base, and sled with acrylic paints, using photograph and pattern as a guide. Allow to dry. To make snow dust on boy's boots, use small amount of white paint and lightly brush boot tops and toes. Using graphite paper, transfer facial features and other details to boy and trace with fine-tipped black paint pen.

Following manufacturer's instructions, varnish boy, sled, and base. Allow to dry. Glue dowels in boy's boots into dowel holes in base.

Draw gold cord through holes in boy's hands, loop around sled runners as shown, and tie into a bow.

Above: Barbara's artwork, decorating, and overall love of color and life come together in her home. Over her left shoulder is a painting of her garden complete with life-size cats.

Top: Adam and Eve are the centerpiece in Barbara's dining room Eden. A variety of hand-carved animals made by family and friends decorate the tall cedar in the corner. A hand-painted Victorian chandelier lights the room.

An Artist for All Seasons

"My paintings became one with nature when I started gardening," says Barbara Strawser, telling of her dual vocations of artist and gardener. "I'm a very seasonal person. When the first crow calls, I begin my paintings of autumn, and I get this passion for pumpkins."

Barbara has a cooperative relationship with the seasons. Winter, spring, summer, and fall nourish her with their colors and motifs; she captures them in her special style of painting for all to enjoy.

The influence of the seasons can be seen in the self-taught artist's array of artwork. A picture of an ice-skating party hangs beside one of a warm summer day on the farm. A lush green garden hides a life-size calico cat and her two friends.

31

Barbara's passion for painting began with high school art classes. "We studied Toulouse-Lautrec one October, and I dressed up like him for Halloween," Barbara reminisces. "I just wanted to paint; that's all I ever wanted to do."

Now the dream is to give her paintings to children in the form of book illustrations. A friend is already working on a story, which features a favorite doll. The doll was named for a dear friend and neighbor, Claudia Hopf, a renowned *scherenschnitte* artist. Claudia always encouraged Barbara, urging her to be patient until her talents were recognized. Just as Barbara was beginning to see how her painting and gardening talents enhanced each other, Claudia moved away. Soon after she left, Barbara found a handmade doll at a craft show, reminding her so much of Claudia that she traded a painting for it.

The doll has a place of honor under one of several trees that Barbara decorates for Christmas. Even though her three children are now grown, her house is filled with playthings. "No small children live here now, but a visitor would think they did," says Barbara, motioning to a tiny tea party under a Fraser fir.

Toward the end of autumn is when Barbara gets the urge to turn her Victorian home in Schaefferstown, Pennsylvania, into a fanciful Christmas kingdom. Clusters of handmade dolls and toys accent every corner. Fresh-cut trees stand ready for her special touch. Dried arrangements of flowers gathered from her garden add holiday color to every room. Folk art carvings from friends find special places of honor as ornaments and centerpieces.

"I arrange my house the way I make paintings,"

Above: Every inch of Barbara's domain reveals her festive approach to life. These lace-trimmed shelves hold family china year-round and colorful hand-molded candy for the holidays.

Right: A few members of Barbara's special doll clan sit beneath a winter scene that she painted on an old board. The subject is Scharf's Bridge, a favorite ice-skating site for the folks near her former home in Straussburg, Pennsylvania.

she explains. "I put things here and there. I'm always rearranging."

Barbara's holiday decorating adds a glow to the year-round look of whimsy pervasive in the turn-of-the-century interior. A tall bushy cedar in the dining room shows Barbara's love of folk art. Nestled among the pungent branches are hand-carved animals of all kinds with a large yellow-beaked eagle on top. Two of the other trees reveal her love for nature another way. They wear bunches of dried materials grown and gathered from Barbara's luxuriant gardens. Miniature sunflower seedpods, orange and burgundy bittersweet, bright golden tansy, and small pinecones hang as if arranged by a flock of chickadees.

"After Christmas I put the trees outside for the birds," Barbara says. "When they've finished with them, I clip each branch back to six or eight inches. I plant the naked tree trunks somewhere in the garden, and in the spring I plant morning glories or sweet peas to climb on them."

When the green foliage and bright blossoms of spring cover the bare gray branches of winter, Barbara can be found with paintbrush in hand, ready to capture yet another cycle of the seasons.

Above: Barbara's paintings glow with her primitive style. Her pictures are seldom restrained by their frames. She often uses the frame surface to extend an element of the picture in paint or in texture, as with the tramp art frame decorated with orange and gold dots and flowers.

Below: Barbara gathered basketsful of dried materials from her garden to decorate this Fraser fir. Claudia, a doll named after a dear friend, sits on an antique tricycle by the tree. Examples of Barbara's painted finishes can be seen on the small chest and cradle under the tree. Long-haired German shepherd Amadeus is much at home among the fanciful colors and objects.

Winter Woodland Vests

You'll be pleased that you invested your time and talents when you complete this enchanting vest ensemble for your child and her bear. Because wool is used instead of felt for the vest and appliqués, the outcome is a first-quality garment with a cozy feel and appeal. With proper care, preferably dry cleaning, the vests will last for years to come.

Child's Vest

Materials:
patterns on page 136
⅓ yard (60"-wide) green wool
½ yard (60"-wide) black wool
½ yard (45"-wide) red plaid cotton or cotton print for lining
wool scraps: red, green, off-white, brown, yellow, light green, purple, lavender
craft glue
sewing threads: red, black
2 black seed beads
1½ yards (1"-wide) red rickrack
1½ yards (1"-wide) red plaid ribbon
1½ yards (½"-wide) decorative ribbon
1½ yards (1"-wide) green rickrack
1 black frog closure

Note: This medium-sized vest fits children 5 to 8 years old. Adjust as needed. Add ½" seam allowances to vest pattern pieces only, except for necklines.

From green wool, cut 2 (7¼" x 3½") pieces for sides of vest (see Placement Diagram). From black wool, cut 1 (16") square for vest back. From lining fabric, cut 2 (7¼" x 3½") pieces for sides and 1 (16") square for vest back.

Transfer patterns for vest fronts to black wool and lining fabric and cut out. Transfer ground patterns for left and right fronts and vest back to green wool and cut out. Transfer appliqué patterns to wool scraps and cut out.

For vest back, fold 16" square of black wool in half. Transfer back neckline pattern to wool and cut out.

With side and bottom raw edges aligned, place a ground piece on bottom of each vest piece as shown in Placement Diagram and baste in place, leaving top edges open.

Referring to pattern, position flower stems and leaves on right vest front and lightly glue in place, tucking ends under top edge of ground piece. Using red thread, make large straightstitches over stems, working from the left side to the right side of each stem. Continue from top to bottom of each stem. Blanket-stitch top edge of ground pieces to vest fronts and back.

Position remaining appliqué pieces on vest fronts as shown, lightly glue in place, and blanket-stitch

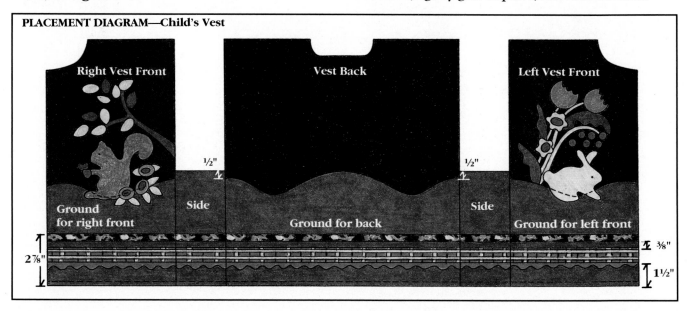

PLACEMENT DIAGRAM—Child's Vest

Right Vest Front · Vest Back · Left Vest Front

Ground for right front · Side · Ground for back · Side · Ground for left front

½" · ½" · ⅜" · 1½" · 2⅞"

around designs, using red thread.

Stitch seed beads to rabbit and squirrel for eyes.

With right sides facing and side and bottom raw edges aligned, stitch green wool side panels to vest fronts and back from large dots to bottom edge (see pattern and Placement Diagram). Lay flat and press vest with a damp towel, pressing seams open. Repeat for lining.

For trim at vest bottom, baste red rickrack to wrong side of 1 long edge of plaid ribbon so that half of the rickrack extends beyond ribbon edge. Referring to Placement Diagram, topstitch plaid and decorative ribbons to vest fronts, sides, and back. Remove basting stitches.

With right sides facing and raw edges aligned, stitch vest fronts to back at shoulder seams. Repeat for lining.

Centering green rickrack on seam line, pin rickrack to right side of vest around each armhole and stitch along center of rickrack. Turn edges under so that half of rickrack extends beyond edges of armhole. Baste; press with damp towel.

With right sides facing and raw edges aligned, stitch lining to vest, leaving armholes open. Clip neckline and corners and turn through armhole. Press.

Turn lining under ½" around each armhole and slipstitch to vest. Remove basting stitches. Press.

Stitch frog closure to vest front at neckline.

Bear's Vest

Materials:
patterns on page 138
¼ yard of black wool
¼ yard of lining fabric
wool scraps: red, green, yellow, purple
craft glue
sewing threads: red, black
19" (1"-wide) red rickrack
19" (½"-wide) decorative ribbon
17" (1"-wide) green rickrack

Note: Vest fits a 14"-16" bear. Adjust as needed. Vest pattern pieces include ½" seam allowances.

Transfer vest front pattern to black wool and lining fabric and cut 1 each for left vest front. Reverse pattern and cut 1 each for right vest front.

Transfer the vest back pattern to black wool and lining fabric and cut 1 each. Transfer the appliqué patterns to fabric scraps and cut out.

Position appliqué designs on vest fronts and back as indicated on patterns, reversing position of front appliqué designs for right vest front. Lightly glue appliqué pieces in place. Blanket-stitch around appliqués, using red thread.

With right sides facing and raw edges aligned, stitch vest fronts to back from large dots to bottom edges. Repeat for lining.

For trim at vest bottom, baste red rickrack to wrong side of 1 long edge of decorative ribbon so that half of rickrack extends beyond ribbon edge. Referring to pattern for placement, topstitch trims to bottom of vest.

With right sides facing and raw edges aligned, stitch lining to vest, leaving armholes open. Clip neckline and corners and turn through armhole.

Stitch rickrack to armholes and then stitch vest to lining as for Child's Vest.

35

Stockings to Hang by the Chimney with Care

Knit one of these wintry stockings as a keepsake for someone special. In country shades of red and green, the stockings can hang along the hearth, waiting to be filled with goodies from St. Nick.

Snowman Stocking

Materials:
chart on page 139
worsted-weight wool: 3 ounces green; 1 ounce each of red, white; small amounts of black, pink
sizes 5 and 7 knitting needles (or size to obtain gauge)
bobbins
stitch holder
tapestry needle
size G crochet hook

GAUGE: 9 sts and 13 rows = 2" in St st on larger needles.

Note: Knitting Abbreviations are on page 153. Stocking is k from the top down. To change colors, wrap old yarn over new so that no holes occur. Since it is best not to carry yarn over more than 3 sts, it may be easier to wind yarn on bobbins while working the chart.

STOCKING: With smaller needles and red, cast on 58 sts. Work in k 1, p 1 ribbing for 10 rows. *Rows 11-24:* Change to larger needles, join green and work in St st for 14 rows (end after p row). *Row 25:* K 33 sts and beg to follow chart. *Rows 26-71:* Continue following chart as est, working colors as indicated. *Row 72-83:* Work 12 rows even in green, ending after p row. Cut green.

HEEL: Join red and work on first 15 sts of row only, put rem 43 sts on holder. *Row 1:* K 15, turn. *Row 2 and subsequent even-numbered rows:* Sl 1, p across. *Row 3:* K 14, turn. *Row 5:* K 13, turn. *Row 7:* K 12, turn. *Row 9:* K 11, turn. *Row 11:* K 10, turn. *Row 13:* K 9, turn. *Row 15:* K 8, turn. *Row 17:* K 7, turn. *Row 19:* K 6, yf, sl 1, yb, turn. *Row 21:* K 7, yf, sl 1, yb, turn. *Row 23:* K 8, yf, sl 1, yb, turn. *Row 25:* K 9, yf, sl 1, yb, turn. *Row 27:* K 10, yf, sl 1, yb turn. *Row 29:* K 11, yf, sl 1, yb, turn. *Row 31:* K 12, yf, sl 1,

yb, turn. *Row 33:* K 13, yf, sl 1, yb, turn. *Row 35:* K 14, yf, sl 1, yb, turn. *Row 36:* Sl 1, p across. Put these sts on holder.

Sl 15 sts from other end of holder onto needle so they can be purled (center 28 sts will be instep). Join red. *Row 1 (wrong side):* P 15. *Row 2 and subsequent even-numbered rows:* Sl 1, k. *Row 3:* P 14, turn. *Row 5:* P 13, turn. *Row 7:* P 12, turn. *Row 9:* P 11, turn. *Row 11:* P 10, turn. *Row 13:* P 9, turn. *Row 15:* P 8, turn. *Row 17:* P 7, turn. *Row 19:* P 6, yb, sl 1, yf, turn. *Row 21:* P 7, yb, sl 1, yf, turn. *Row 23:* P 8, yb, sl 1, yf, turn. *Row 25:* P 9, yb, sl 1, yf, turn. *Row 27:* P 10, yb, sl 1, yf, turn. *Row 29:* P 11, yb, sl 1, yf, turn. *Row 31:* P 12, yb, sl 1, yf, turn. *Row 33:* P 13, yb, sl 1, yf, turn. *Row 35:* P 14, yb, sl 1, yf, turn. *Row 36:* Sl 1, k across. Cut red.

INSTEP: *Row 1:* Put all 58 sts on needle, join green and k. *Row 2:* P across. *Row 3:* K 13, ssk, k 2 tog, k 24, ssk, k 2 tog, k 13. *Row 4:* P across. *Row 5:* K 12, ssk, k 2 tog, k 22, ssk, k 2 tog, k 12. *Row 6:* P across. Work even in St st for 4½" from end of heel ending after a p row. Cut green.

TOE: *Row 1:* Join red and k. *Row 2:* P across. *Row 3:* K 11, ssk, k 2 tog, k 20, ssk, k 2 tog, k 11. *Row 4:* P across. *Row 5:* K 10, ssk, k 2 tog, k 18, ssk, k 2 tog, k 10. *Row 6:* P across. *Row 7:* K 9, ssk, k 2 tog, k 16, ssk, k 2 tog, k 9. *Row 8:* P across. *Row 9:* K 8, ssk, k 2 tog, k 14, ssk, k 2 tog, k 8. *Row 10:* P across. *Row 11:* K 7, ssk, k 2 tog, k 12, ssk, k 2 tog, k 7. *Row 12:* P across. *Row 13:* K 6, ssk, k 2 tog, k 10, ssk, k 2 tog, k 6. *Row 14:* P across. *Row 15:* K 5, ssk, k 2 tog, k 8, ssk, k 2 tog, k 5. Graft toe sts tog. Weave in ends.

FINISHING: With black, make 4 French knots as indicated on chart for buttons and eyes. Duplicate-stitch cheeks with pink as indicated on chart. Embroider mouth with 1 strand of red. To make pom-pom: Wind red loosely around 2 fingers about 10 times. Slip a piece of yarn around loops and tie tightly. Cut loops and trim even. Sew pom-pom to top of hat.

To make scarf: With red and smaller needles, cast on 3 sts. Work even in garter st (k every row) for 4". Bind off. Rep for other half of scarf but bind off after 3". Tack scarf pieces to snowman's neck. Cross shorter piece over longer piece and tack together (see photograph). Tie short pieces of yarn through stitches on ends of scarf for fringe.

With tapestry needle and matching yarn, sew stocking seam.

HANGER: With crochet hook and green, chain 15 or desired length. Work a slip stitch in 2nd chain from hook and in each chain to end. Fold in half and tack to stocking.

Tree-and-Snowflake Stocking

Materials:
chart on page 139
worsted-weight wool: 3 ounces red; 2 ounces each of green, white
4 each sizes 5 and 7 double-pointed knitting needles (or size to obtain gauge)
stitch markers
yarn needle
size G crochet hook

GAUGE: 9 sts and 13 rows = 2" in St st on larger needles.

Note: Knitting Abbreviations are on page 153. Stocking is k from the top down. To change colors, wrap old yarn over new so that no holes occur. Carry colors not in use loosely across the back of work. To prevent a ridge of stretched sts, move 1 or 2 sts from each needle to the next every few rnds. Move the same number of sts in the same direction each time.

STOCKING: With smaller needles and red, cast 56 sts onto 3 needles (18-19-19). Sl a marker on needle after last st to indicate end of rnd. Connect and k in the rnd. *Rnds 1-5:* K around. *Rnd 6:* * Yo, k 2 tog, rep from * around. *Rnds 7-9:* K around. *Rnds 10 and 11:* Join green and follow chart, rep indicated portion of design for pat. *Rnd 12:* Fold top of stocking over at yo rnd (with cast-on edge inside stocking), * place 1 st from cast-on edge on needle and k 2 tog (regular st and cast-on st), rep from * around to fasten top hem of stocking. *Rnds 13-38:* Change to larger needles, join white and continue following chart as est. *Rnds 39-67:* Rep rnds 10-38 of chart. *Rnds 68-87:* Rep rnds 10-29 of chart. Cut white. *Rnds 88 and 89:* With red, k 2 rnds. Cut red.

HEEL: Arrange sts so first 14 and last 14 sts are on 1 needle. With green, work back and forth on these heel sts as follows: *Row 1:* K 28, turn. *Row 2:* Sl 1, p 26, turn. *Row 3:* Sl 1, k 25, turn. *Row 4:* Sl 1, p 24, turn. *Row 5:* Sl 1, k 23, turn. *Row 6:* Sl 1, p 22, turn. *Rows 7-18:* Continue in this manner, sl the first st and k or p 1 less st than previous row. *Row 19:* Sl 1, k 11, turn. *Row 20:* Sl 1, p 10, yb, sl 1, yf, turn. *Row 21:* Sl 1, k 10, yf, sl 1, yb, turn. *Row 22:* Sl 1, p 11, yb, sl 1, yf, turn. *Row 23:* Sl 1, k 12, yf, sl 1, yb, turn. *Row 24:* Sl 1, p 13, yb, sl 1, yf, turn. *Row 25:* Sl 1, k 14, yf, sl 1, yb, turn. Continue in this manner, which wraps yarn around first and last sts, and k or p 1 more st each row. End with sl 1, k 26, yf, sl 1, yb, turn. Sl 1, p 27. Cut green.

INSTEP: On right side and at right edge of heel sts, join red. Arrange sts on 3 needles and work in the rnd. Sl a marker on needle to indicate beg of rnd. *Rnds 1 and 2:* K around. *Rnd 3:* (K 2 tog, k 24, ssk) twice. *Rnd 4:* K around. *Rnd 5:* (K 2 tog, k 22, ssk) twice. *Rnd 6 and following:* Work even in St st for 5". Cut red.

TOE: Join green and k 1 rnd. *Rnd 2:* (K 2 tog, k 20, ssk) twice. *Rnd 3:* K around. *Rnd 4:* (K 2 tog, k 18, ssk) twice. *Rnd 5:* K around. *Rnd 6:* (K 2 tog, k 16, ssk) twice. *Rnds 7-14:* Continue in this manner, dec as est each edge every other row. End with (k 2 tog, k 8, ssk) twice. Graft toe sts tog. Weave in ends.

HANGER: With crochet hook and green, chain 15 (or desired length). Work a slip stitch in 2nd chain from hook and in each chain to end. Fold in half and tack to stocking.

Hearts and Flowers for the Home

Even if you don't consider yourself an artist, it won't take you long to master the simple technique of stenciling. With the designs featured on these accessories, you can try your own combinations to embellish items you already have on hand or to create custom-made gifts for friends.

Materials for *all* stenciled projects:
stencil patterns on page 140
frosted mylar
craft knife
clear tape
masking tape
acrylic fabric paints: red, green, blue
3 stencil brushes

Wash and press all fabrics except heavy canvas before cutting. To mark center of fabric, fold in half horizontally and then vertically; finger-press.

Working on a hard surface, trace stencil pattern onto frosted side of mylar, making a separate stencil for each paint color. Cut stencils on shiny side of mylar.

Mix and match all or parts of the stenciled designs. Use clear tape to correct cutting errors or block out portions of design. If desired, practice stenciling on paper before stenciling fabric.

Tape fabric to a smooth work surface. Center and stencil design, starting with largest color area and working with 1 color at a time. Allow each color to dry several hours. To heat-set design on fabric only, press fabric on wrong side, using a press cloth and a hot, dry iron.

Gift Bags

Materials for 1 bag:
1 paper bag
portable flat surface (cake pan, tray, or box)

Note: Do not use a bag with a shiny surface.

Open bag and insert cake pan, tray, box, or any smooth, flat surface to stabilize bag. Center and stencil design onto bag, using desired paints and stencil brushes. Allow to dry.

Pillow Sham

Materials for 1 pillow sham:
½ yard (45"-wide) unbleached muslin
1⅝ yards (45"-wide) red cotton fabric
threads to match fabrics
14"-square pillow form

Note: All seam allowances are ½".

For pillow front, cut a 14½" square of muslin. Center and stencil design onto front of muslin square, using stencil brushes and desired paints. Allow to dry.

For pillow back, cut 2 (10½" x 14½") pieces of muslin. On 1 long edge of each piece, fold under 1" twice and hem. Overlap hemmed edges and baste together to form a 14½" square.

For ruffle, from red fabric, make a 5¼"-wide continuous bias strip, piecing as needed to equal 85". With wrong sides facing, fold strip in half lengthwise and press. Run a gathering thread along long edges and pull to gather. With right sides facing and raw edges aligned, stitch ruffle to pillow front, adjusting gathers as needed.

With right sides facing, raw edges aligned, and ruffle toward center, stitch pillow front to back, sewing along stitching line of ruffle. Clip corners and turn. Insert pillow form.

Right: Stenciled white or brown paper bags make quick gift wraps for those hard-to-package presents. These versatile stencil designs may be mixed and matched in many ways.

Place Mats

Materials for 4 place mats:
1⅜ yards (36"-wide) heavy canvas
¾ yard (36"-wide) cotton flannel to match
  canvas
thread to match fabric

Note: Canvas shown in photograph is #10 awning canvas.

Cut 8 (12" x 16") rectangles from canvas and 4 (11½" x 15½") rectangles from flannel.

Referring to photograph and allowing ¾" for border fringe, center and stencil designs onto 4 of the rectangles, using desired paints and stencil brushes. Allow to dry.

Center 1 flannel rectangle on 1 unstenciled rectangle. Stack 1 stenciled rectangle (design side up) on flannel and pin all 3 pieces together. Machine-stitch around rectangles through all layers, ¾" from edge. Fringe raw edges of place mat top and backing by pulling threads parallel to stitching line for ½". Repeat to make 3 more place mats.

Coasters

Materials for 6 coasters:
⅜ yard (36"-wide) heavy canvas
¼ yard (36"-wide) cotton flannel to match
  canvas
thread to match fabric

Note: Canvas shown in photograph is #10 awning canvas.

Cut 12 (5") squares from canvas and 6 (4¾") squares from flannel.

Referring to photograph and allowing ½" for border fringe, center and stencil designs onto 6 of the squares, using desired paints and stencil brushes. Allow to dry.

Center 1 flannel rectangle on 1 unstenciled rectangle. Stack 1 stenciled rectangle (design side up) on flannel and pin all 3 pieces together. Machine-stitch around squares through all layers, ½" from edge. Fringe raw edges of coaster top and backing by pulling threads parallel to stitching line for ¼". Repeat to make 5 more coasters.

Left: These brightly graphic pillow shams use daisy, tulip, and heart motifs as separate, yet interchangeable, stencil designs.

Feathered Friends

Inexpensive materials and quick designs allow you to make these cross-stitched bird wreaths for a song. While they will look at home among the branches of your Christmas tree, the ornaments will also add country styling to your walls or windows year-round.

Materials for 1 ornament:
charts and color key on page 139
9" square of 14-count white Aida cloth
embroidery floss (see color key)
3¼"-diameter circle of self-adhesive mounting
   board
craft knife
4"-diameter vine wreath
1 yard (¼"-wide) red satin picot ribbon
hot-glue gun and glue sticks
10" gold cord

Using 2 strands of floss, center and work desired bird design on Aida cloth according to chart.

Center wrong side of completed cross-stitch on self-adhesive mounting board and press firmly. Cut away excess fabric. Set circle aside.

Referring to photograph, wrap ribbon 7 or 8 times around vine wreath. Glue ends of ribbon to back of wreath. Make a small bow with remaining ribbon; then center and glue bow to bottom front of wreath.

Center wreath on right side of mounted cross-stitch and glue in place. Hold wreath securely in place until glue dries.

For hanger, fold gold cord in half and glue ends to back of mounting board.

A Prim and Proper Christmas Kitten

Your child will delight in finding this properly attired cotton kitten under the Christmas tree. And you'll be happy that her cloth body and apparel require only basic sewing and painting skills.

Materials:
patterns on page 144
tracing paper
¼ yard (45"-wide) gray cotton
½ yard (45"-wide) muslin
½ yard (45"-wide) Christmas miniprint
threads to match fabrics
polyester stuffing
clear acrylic spray
acrylic paints: light green, white, gray, brick red
small paintbrush
pink pencil or crayon
black fine-tip permanent marker
quilting threads: cream, gray
1½ yards (½"-wide) lace
1 (¼") snap set
1¼ yards (⅛"-wide) ivory ribbon
2" artificial holly trim (optional)

Note: Add ¼" seam allowances to all pattern pieces.

Using tracing paper, transfer patterns and markings to fabrics and cut out.

With right sides facing and raw edges aligned, stitch 2 arm pieces together, leaving open as indicated on pattern. Clip curves and turn. Repeat for other arm, legs, tail, and ears. Stuff tail firmly, turn raw edges under ¼", and slipstitch opening closed. For arms and legs, stuff to joint line on pattern; then topstitch along joint line. Do not stuff past stitching. Do not stuff ears.

For ears, run a gathering thread along raw edge of each ear and pull to measure 1¼".

With right sides facing and raw edges aligned, baste arms, legs, and ears to body back where indicated on pattern. With right sides facing, raw edges aligned, and arms and ears inside, stitch body front to body back, catching arms and ears in seam and leaving bottom of body open. Clip curves, turn, and stuff firmly. Slipstitch opening closed. Reinforce body

bottom by topstitching ⅛" from edge. Slipstitch tail to bottom center of body back.

Lightly spray face and paws with acrylic spray to prevent acrylic paints from bleeding into fabric. Allow to dry. Transfer facial features and paw pads to body from patterns. Referring to patterns and photograph, paint face and paws using acrylic paints. Highlight facial features with white acrylic paint. Use pink pencil or crayon to lightly shade cheeks. Use black permanent marker to lightly draw dots in whisker areas and outlines around facial features. For whiskers, using cream quilting thread, insert needle on 1 side of face below nose and pull out on other, trimming thread to 1¼" on both sides. Repeat to make 5 more sets of whiskers. Make 2 sets of eyebrows in same manner.

To make toes on paws, use gray quilting thread to make small backstitches, looping thread from back to front through stuffing and over edge of limb and pulling thread tightly.

For dress back, cut 1 dress piece in half along fold line. With right sides facing and raw edges aligned, stitch back pieces together at center back from bottom edge to dot. Press seam open. To finish back opening, turn remaining seam allowance under and topstitch to make a narrow hem. With right sides facing and raw edges aligned, stitch dress front to back at shoulder and side seams. Press seams open.

For sleeve, cut a 3¼" piece of lace. Turn raw edges of long straight edge of sleeve under ¼" for hem. Lay lace over hem on wrong side of sleeve and topstitch lace to hem so that lace extends below sleeve. With right sides facing and raw edges aligned, stitch sides of sleeve together. Run a hand-gathering stitch around top of sleeve and gather to fit dress armhole. With right sides facing and raw edges and seams aligned, insert sleeve into armhole and stitch to dress. Repeat for other sleeve.

For neckline, turn raw edge under ¼". Cut an 8½" piece of lace. Stitch lace to neckline in same manner as for sleeves. Run a hand-gathering stitch around neckline and gather slightly. Secure threads. Sew snap to top back of dress.

To hem dress, turn raw edge under ¼" twice and topstitch.

For pantalettes, turn bottom raw edge of 1 pantalette piece under ¼". Cut a 7½" piece of lace. Stitch lace to bottom of pantalette in same manner as for sleeves. Repeat for other pantalette piece. With right sides facing and raw edges aligned, fold 1 pantalette piece in half along fold line. Stitch inner leg seam. Repeat for other pantalette piece. With

right sides facing and raw edges aligned, stitch pantalette pieces together along front inseam only, leaving back inseam open as indicated on pattern to fit around tail. To finish opening, turn remaining seam allowance under at back inseam and topstitch to make a narrow hem.

Turn top edge of pantalettes under ¼" twice and topstitch to form casing. To make drawstring, cut an 18" piece of ribbon. Attach a small safety pin to 1 end of ribbon and pull ribbon through casing.

For apron back, cut 1 apron piece in half along fold line. With right sides facing and raw edges aligned, stitch apron front to backs at shoulder and side seams. Turn raw edges under ¼" along neckline, center back, and armholes, and topstitch. Turn bottom edge under ¼" twice and topstitch. For ties, cut 2 (5") pieces of ribbon. Tack 1 end of 1 piece of ribbon to 1 side at top of neckline. Repeat for other side.

For bonnet, cut 1 (1½" x 7½") piece of muslin for brim. Turn ends under ¼" and topstitch. With wrong sides facing, fold strip in half lengthwise. Turn long edges under ¼" and press. Topstitch long edges together close to edge. Press.

Turn straight edge of bonnet under ¼" and topstitch. Repeat for curved edge.

Run a hand-gathering stitch around curved edge and gather to fit brim. Slipstitch gathered edge of bonnet to brim, leaving openings for ears as indicated on pattern. Hand-gather bottom straight edge of bonnet to measure 3¾". Secure thread.

For ties, cut 2 (6") pieces of ribbon. Tack 1 end of 1 piece of ribbon to 1 side of bonnet at brim. Repeat for other side. If desired, tack holly to side of bonnet.

Sculpt a Wire Wreath

Materials:
patterns on page 133
wire cutters
1 roll (18-gauge) galvanized wire
20 (8-mm) red beads: wood, plastic, or glass
needle-nosed pliers
black marker
1 roll (24-gauge) galvanized wire
1 yard (1½"-wide) plaid ribbon

Note: The 18-gauge wire is used as the base for each shape. The 24-gauge wire is wrapped around the 18-gauge wire.

For outer circle, cut 1 (30") length of 18-gauge wire. Thread 12 beads onto wire. Using pliers, shape wire into a circle, looping ends of wire over each other and crimping to close. To make inner circle, cut 1 (17") length of 18-gauge wire and thread remaining 8 beads onto it. Shape wire and crimp ends as above.

Using black marker, make 12 evenly spaced dots around outer circle. Beginning between any 2 dots, wrap 24-gauge wire around 18-gauge wire to first dot. Slide 1 bead to dot and wrap wire once over bead to secure. Continue wrapping wire around circle to next dot and secure next bead. Repeat until all beads are secured. Wrap wire over starting point and cut off excess.

On inner circle, mark 8 dots as above and repeat to secure beads.

To make a heart, cut 1 (10") length of 18-gauge wire. Referring to heart pattern, use pliers to shape wire into a heart. Wrap 24-gauge wire several times around 2 wires at top center of heart to form joint. Continue wrapping wire around heart. Secure wire over starting point and cut off excess. Repeat to make 3 more hearts.

To make a 3-loop figure, cut 1 (16") length of 18-gauge wire. Referring to 3-loop pattern, use pliers to shape wire into a 3-loop figure. Wrap 24-gauge wire several times as shown in 3-loop pattern to form Joint 1. Continue wrapping wire around center loop. Secure wire over starting point and cut off excess. Form Joint 2 in same manner. Continue wrapping wire around right loop, ending at Joint 1. Secure wire and cut off excess. Form Joint 3 in same manner. Continue wrapping wire around left loop, ending at Joint 1. Secure wire and cut off excess. Repeat to make 3 more 3-loop figures.

Referring to Placement Diagram, use wrapping/joining technique described above to first attach hearts and then 3-loop figures between outer and inner circles with 24-gauge wire. Adjust to fit if necessary. (Center loop of 3-loop figures will extend approximately ½" beyond outer circle.)

For center of wreath, cut 1 (10") length of 18-gauge wire and follow directions for heart used in wreath. For 1-loop figure, cut 1 (8") length of 18-gauge wire. Referring to 1-loop pattern, use pliers to shape wire into loop. Wrap wire as described above to form joints and attach heart as indicated on 1-loop pattern. Secure wire and cut off excess. Using a small piece of wire, center and attach top of 1-loop figure directly under 3-loop figure (see photograph).

For hanger, thread ribbon through loop at top (see photograph) and tie ends together.

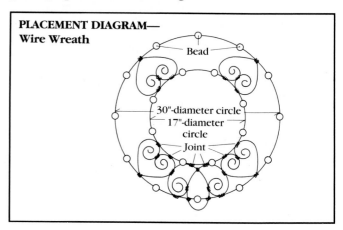

PLACEMENT DIAGRAM—Wire Wreath

Bead

30"-diameter circle
17"-diameter circle

Joint

Above: Red and green duplicate stitches complement the deep black and bright red wool of a purchased sweater and mittens. For Tassel Earring instructions, see photograph on page 65.

Quick and Cozy Winter Woolens

Who would guess that these festive Christmas accessories with the hand-crafted charm of knitting are really purchased garments embellished with duplicate stitching!

Materials:
charts and color key on page 142
purchased black sweater
purchased red mittens
straight pins
3-strand Persian yarn (see color key)
tapestry needle

Center tree design on top front of sweater or mittens, marking with straight pins. It is preferable to mark garments while they are on the body, since the centers may change from when the garments are lying flat.

For duplicate stitching, thread tapestry needle with 4 strands of yarn, each 20"-24" in length. Starting from the wrong side of the piece, pull the needle up through the stitch below the one to be covered, leaving about a 2" tail of yarn. Pass the needle from right to left under the stitch above the one to be covered (see Diagram 1). Reinsert the needle into the stitch through which you originally pulled the needle (see Diagram 2).

Follow the chart and color key to complete tree on sweater front and mittens, pulling stitches carefully so that the embroidery covers the knitted stitches but does not pucker fabric. When finished, weave the yarn tail through several stitches on the wrong side of the fabric.

For neckline and cuffs of sweater, position and work design according to chart, being careful not to pull stitches too tight. Repeat for mitten cuffs.

All About Duplicate Stitch

With its simple execution, the duplicate stitch has been for years the knitter's best kept secret. Once used only to add detail when the knitter did not want to change yarns frequently, this stitch is now a popular way to give purchased garments a hand-knitted look quickly.

The duplicate stitch gets its name because it duplicates the structure of the knitted stockinette stitch, the smooth, flat V stitch often used in making sweaters.

If a duplicate-stitch design is charted on the rectangular graph paper specifically made for knitting, then the finished piece will be in the same proportion as the graph. However, if the design is charted on square graph paper designed for even-weave fabrics, then the graph will appear taller and narrower than the finished stitching. Therefore, you cannot substitute needlepoint or cross-stitch charts for duplicate-stitch or knitting charts.

DUPLICATE STITCHING

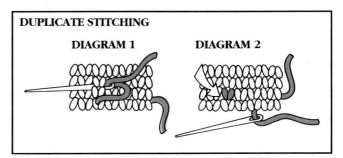

DIAGRAM 1	DIAGRAM 2

Above: They started out as business partners, but over the years they have become dear friends. From left: Jan Patek, Linda Brannock, and Gerry Kimmel.

Snowbound Is a State of Mind

Snowbound is not necessarily a weather condition. It can be a state of mind. Stoke the furnace, put on the soup, and imagine a full day of quilting—makes you smile, doesn't it?

Avid quilters look for every opportunity to put the ordinary world aside and enter the "real" world of quilting, even during the busy holidays. The thought that all the outdoor chores, all the errands, and all the last-minute shopping will be put on hold for a few days of uninterrupted quilting has undeniable allure. The quilt design group known as Red Wagon, of Liberty, Missouri, understands this temptation very well.

"Snowbound means we can quit working for awhile. There's nothing to do but check the wood stove and quilt," says designer Jan Patek.

It was appropriate, then, that the first collaboration of the three Red Wagon designers was a quilt inspired by winter wonderlands, *Snowbound.*

Jan made a Christmas quilt for her family, mixing some of designer Gerry Kimmel's patterns with her own. She took it by Gerry's quilt shop. It was the beginning of the first quilt pattern booklet produced by Jan and Gerry, with help from fellow quilter Linda Brannock. Since pulling together their first publication, they have published *Pioneer Spirit, Down the Road a Piece, Collections I, Collections II,* and *Noah.*

"We get together and the ideas just snowball," says Linda. The three meet once a week or so for half a day at Gerry's studio, which is filled with fabrics for experimentation. At first they met for all-day sessions, but they generated too many ideas and were just worn out.

"Jan has an immense amount of energy. Gerry and I are a little more laid back," says Linda. Jan considers this difference in energy level important to their designs, saying, "Both the busy and relaxed aspects are evident in our work."

With three personalities and design interests to

consider, it would seem that conflicts might arise. But that doesn't fit into Red Wagon.

"We grow from each other's ideas instead of trying to top one another," says Jan. "It's just fun! It's wonderful to make a living at something I love,"

Gerry adds. "We all inspire each other."

"We started out as a business. We all share an appreciation of primitive style, folk art, and muted colors. That was the basis of our acquaintance, but it has turned into a really deep friendship," says Jan.

Below: Snowbound *is the fruit of Gerry, Linda, and Jan's first efforts. For information about ordering the* Snowbound *pattern book or other books from Red Wagon, see the source listing on page 154.*

Snowbound-Inspired Stocking and Tree Skirt

Outline-quilting and hand-appliquéd fabric pieces in folk art shapes lend country charm to this snowman tree skirt and stocking from Red Wagon.

Snowman Stocking

Materials:
patterns on page 146
tracing paper
water-soluble marker
¾ yard (45"-wide) cotton print for stocking
18" x 30" piece of thin quilt batting
¾ yard (45"-wide) cotton print for lining
contrasting cotton fabric scraps for appliqué
   pieces
threads to match fabrics
cream quilting thread

Note: Patterns include ¼" seam allowances. If desired, fabric scraps for appliqué pieces may be dyed with tan commercial dye to give cloth an aged appearance.

Using tracing paper, enlarge and transfer stocking pattern to cotton print and cut 1. Reverse and cut 1 more. Repeat for batting and lining fabric. Transfer appliqué patterns to contrasting fabric scraps and cut out as indicated on patterns. Using water-soluble marker, transfer all pattern markings to fabric.

Referring to patterns and photograph for placement, turn edges of appliqué pieces under ¼" and hand-appliqué to stocking front. For snowman, appliqué body, then scarf, then hat; for dog, appliqué ears, then tail and body.

Baste batting to wrong side of each stocking piece. Outline-quilt around appliqué pieces as follows: For snowman, outline-quilt ¼" inside and ⅛" outside edges. For dog, outline-quilt ⅛" outside edges. For stars, outline-quilt ¼" inside edges; then ⅛" and ⅜" outside edges.

With right sides facing and raw edges aligned, stitch stocking pieces together, leaving top open. Repeat for lining pieces. Clip curves and trim seams. Turn stocking; do not turn lining.

Slip lining inside stocking, aligning seams. To make cuff, fold lining down over top edge of stocking, turn raw edge of lining under ¼", and slipstitch in place.

Below: The stylish snowman, caroling pup, and primary-colored stars from Red Wagon's Snowbound *quilt give this stocking its old-time country feel.*

Left: Jaunty snowmen with their mufflers askew nestle among calico trees.

To make loop for hanging, cut a 1" x 6" rectangle from stocking scrap. With right sides facing, fold in half lengthwise and stitch long edges together. Turn. Fold in half to make a loop. Turn ends under ¼" and tack ends inside stocking at right seam.

Snowman Tree Skirt

Materials:
patterns and placement diagram on page 146
tracing paper
water-soluble marker
1½ yards (45"-wide) cotton print for skirt top
1½ yards (45"-wide) checked cotton for backing
contrasting cotton fabric scraps for appliqué
  pieces
43" square of thin quilt batting
cream quilting thread
black embroidery floss
⅔ yard contrasting cotton for bias binding
threads to match fabrics

Note: Patterns include ¼" seam allowance. If desired, fabric scraps for appliqué pieces may be dyed with tan commercial dye to give cloth an aged appearance.

Using tracing paper, enlarge and transfer skirt panel pattern to skirt top and backing fabrics and cut out as indicated. Transfer appliqué patterns to contrasting fabric scraps and cut out. Using water-soluble marker, transfer pattern markings to fabric.

With right sides facing and raw edges aligned, stitch 6 skirt top panels together, leaving first and last panel unjoined. Repeat for backing. Use backing as a pattern to cut out batting.

Referring to Placement Diagram, turn edges of appliqué pieces under ¼" and hand-appliqué to skirt top. Appliqué tree trunk first and then appliqué tree.

Stack backing, right side down; batting; and skirt top, right side up. Baste.

Outline-quilt around appliqué pieces, ¼" inside edges; then ⅛" and ⅜" outside edges.

Outline-quilt around tree skirt, ½" and 1" from bottom edge. Trim excess batting from all edges of skirt.

Referring to snowman pattern, use 3 strands of black embroidery floss to make French knots for mouths and Xs or French knots for buttons.

To make binding, cut 1" bias strips from contrasting fabric, piecing as needed to make 3⅓ yards. With right sides facing and raw edges aligned, stitch bias strip along all edges of tree skirt. Clip curves. Fold bias strip to skirt back. Turn raw edges under ¼" and slipstitch to skirt back, mitering corners.

49

Wings of Freedom

Perch this patriotic eagle on your Christmas tree with pride.

Materials for 1 ornament:
patterns on page 148
tracing paper
scrap of unbleached muslin
scrap of red pindot
threads to match fabrics
scrap of thin quilt batting
navy blue embroidery floss
embroidery needle
6" (⅛"-wide) red ribbon

Note: Patterns include ¼" seam allowances.

Using tracing paper, transfer patterns to fabric and batting and cut out.

Baste 1 batting body piece to wrong side of 1 fabric body piece. With right sides facing and raw edges aligned, stitch body front to body back, leaving small opening in seam for turning. Trim batting from seam. Clip curves and turn. Slipstitch opening closed.

Repeat for shield and wings.

Referring to patterns for placement, tack shield to body front and wings to body back. Using 3 strands of embroidery floss, work French knots at dots on shield through all layers.

To make hanger, thread embroidery needle with red ribbon. Referring to pattern, pull ribbon from back of left wing to front; then push from front of right wing to back. Knot ribbon ends to secure.

Below: Create a pair of facing eagles by reversing the body pattern piece so that the beak faces in the opposite direction.

Left: Kim's husband, Todd, takes care of the business side of their enterprise, Kim's Characters. "I'm math and science; she's arts and crafts," explains Todd, who works in an environmental laboratory. "But my biggest job is to keep our little girl, Cassidy, out of Kim's way."

"Gourdeous" Santas

A few years ago, Kim Skeen came across some gourds stored in her aunt's basement. Most people think of birdhouses for martins when they see the dried tan vine-fruit. Not Kim. She saw the long curving top and the bulging bottom and thought of just one thing.

"When I saw the nice fat round shape of the gourd," Kim says, "I thought, 'That's just what Santa Claus should look like!'"

Now, at the young age of 25, Kim has already built quite a reputation as a folk artist. "I guess I've gotten pretty popular lately," she says humbly of her recent gallery shows, which have been held as far from her Knoxville, Tennessee, home as New Jersey and West Virginia. She paints Santas, animals, and scenes on "birdhouse" gourds, long-necked gourds, "world-sized" gourds, and hen-egg gourds. Long since finished with the small basement supply, Kim buys some gourds at flea markets and grows some herself.

Her aunt, Bernice Sellars, a painter, has had a big influence on Kim. When Kim was a little girl, she loved to draw and paint the animals at her aunt's farm. After Kim graduated from high school, she and her mother, Janet McCarter, started a business together. Her mother stitched up canvas Santas and Kim painted them.

"I've always loved whimsical things," Kim says. "I think it's reflected in my work." Her husband, Todd, agrees, "Her work is all over our house. It's a good 'at-home' feeling to be surrounded by her art. It's just comfortable."

And her art is sure to endure. As Kim says, "They used gourds in biblical times to dip water, so they've been around for a long time."

Above: Kim has collected cloth and wooden Santas for years and especially loves the roly-poly ones. Her painted gourds are reminiscent of those rounded versions, but no two of her Santas ever look the same. "Each one has a different personality," she beams. "I don't do assembly-line work. Every Santa is one of a kind."

Right: Kim tries out her artistic talents in a number of media. Unlike the red roly-poly canvas Santa in front, the clay-faced Father Christmas with the fur-trimmed suit combines her painting, sewing, and sculpture skills. The wagon was handmade by Todd's grandfather.

A Sprightly Trio

Details, details! It's the details that make this trio of busy elves so adorable. And the details are up to you—buttons, bows, sequins, pom-poms. Add your own frills to the elf's basic design.

Materials for 1 elf:
patterns on page 142–143
tracing paper
fabric scraps: muslin, white felt, solid and
    miniprint Christmas fabrics
threads to match fabrics
fine-tipped permanent markers: black, red,
    pink
pink crayon
assorted trims, beads, and sequins
polyester stuffing
craft glue
1 (½"-diameter) pom-pom
scraps of yarn, metallic thread, or pearl cotton

Note: Patterns include ¼" seam allowances.

Using tracing paper, transfer patterns for desired elf to contrasting fabrics and cut out.

For all elves, transfer desired facial details to face piece, tracing eyes and freckles with black marker, and nose and mouth with red or pink marker or crayon. Lightly shade cheeks with pink crayon. Referring to pattern, position and baste face on body.

For elf with either apron, hem apron bottom and sides (but not armholes), and decorate hemline with trims or topstitching. Referring to photograph, place apron on body front with straps positioned under face piece. Machine-appliqué around face with cream thread and around apron neckline and armholes with thread to match apron. Embellish apron front with assorted trims and beads. Pin hemmed edges of apron skirt to center of body front to prevent catching in seams when joining front and back.

For elf with belt and collar, cut a ½" x 6" strip of contrasting fabric. With matching thread, machine-appliqué belt to body front 1¼" above bottom edge of body. Referring to photograph, glue collar to body front below face. Embellish body front and collar with assorted trims, beads, and bows.

For arms, with right sides facing and raw edges aligned, fold 1 arm piece in half widthwise and stitch edges parallel to fold together. Turn. Turn under ¼" on 1 open end and run a gathering thread around opening. With raw edges aligned and referring to pattern for placement, pin other end of arm to right side of body front. Repeat for other arm.

With right sides facing, raw edges aligned, and arms toward center of body, stitch body front and back together, catching arms in seams and leaving bottom edge open.

For legs, with right sides facing and raw edges aligned, stitch 2 leg pieces together, leaving top edge open. Repeat for other leg. Turn legs, stuff firmly, and baste opening closed. Stuff body firmly. Referring to pattern, insert legs into opening at bottom of body. Turn seam allowances under and whipstitch opening closed, attaching legs to bottom of body.

For hands, with right sides facing and raw edges aligned, stitch 2 hand pieces together, leaving open as indicated on pattern. Turn and stuff. Repeat for other hand.

Stuff 1 arm. Referring to photograph, insert 1 hand, with thumb pointed upward, ¼" into 1 arm opening. Gather wrist tightly and slipstitch to hand. Repeat for other hand and arm.

For cap, with right sides facing and raw edges aligned, stitch cap pieces together, leaving straight edge open. Turn cap and lightly stuff. Turn raw edges under ⅛" and slipstitch to head. Cut a ¼" x 6" piece of fabric or trim and glue around bottom edge of hat. Referring to photograph, attach assorted trims, sequins, and bows to cap. Glue pom-pom to the tip of the cap.

For hair, cut 2 (8") pieces of yarn. Add an 8" length of gold metallic thread, if desired, for highlights. Holding pieces together as 1, wrap yarn around 2 fingers 3 times and tie in center with thread. Repeat to make 8 "curls." Glue curls around top of elf's face.

Refer to the photograph to finish elf. Tack the assorted trims to hands; glue arms to side of body so that they point outward; or tie the assorted trims to a 6" piece of pearl cotton and tack yarn ends to center of each hand.

Papier-mâché Santas

An outer layer of papier mâché gives these two Santas texture and depth. The slick coating of texture paste seals the papier mâché so that it won't absorb the paint. A final finish of antiquing mud gives the Santas an old-time look.

Underneath, both are simple surprises. The Santa Cone Ornament uses a bathroom tissue tube as a base. An oyster shell gives each Santa necklace a different beard.

Santa Cone Ornament

Materials:
bathroom tissue tube
masking tape
papier mâché
modeling tool
150-grit sandpaper
texture paste
electric drill with ¼" bit
small paintbrush
ceramic paints: flesh, black, white, antique
  white, brick red
paint thinner
antiquing mud (also called art mud)
twine
dried moss, holly berries, pine twigs, or other
  decorative winter greenery

Note: Papier mâché takes at least 48 hours to dry and must be thoroughly dry before paint is applied. Texture paste and antiquing mud are available at local craft stores.

To make ornament base, cut a 4" length from bathroom tissue tube. Using ruler and pencil, mark a line around circumference of tube, 1½" from bottom. Slit tube from bottom to pencil line at ¼" intervals to form cardboard "fringe" (see Diagram 1). To make a cone shape, pinch fringe into a point and tape to secure (see Diagram 2).

Following manufacturer's instructions, prepare papier mâché. Apply a thin layer of papier mâché to entire outside surface of cone and 1" inside top of cone. Allow to dry.

Using papier mâché and modeling tool and referring to Diagram 3, make a ⅜"-wide band around top of cone for hatband; also form beard and hair. Apply a layer of papier mâché thick enough to build facial features. Using modeling tool, make shallow indentations for eyes and mouth. Referring to Diagram 4, shape nose by forming a small elongated triangle from remaining papier mâché and pressing it lightly onto middle of face, blending edges smoothly. Allow to dry.

To smooth band and face (not beard or hair), lightly sand with sandpaper. Following manufacturer's instructions, seal entire cone with texture paste. Allow to dry.

Using electric drill, drill a small hole just under band on each side of cone. Referring to photograph, paint cone.

When paint is dry, make a thin wash with equal parts paint thinner and antiquing mud and paint over entire ornament. Wipe off excess. Allow to dry.

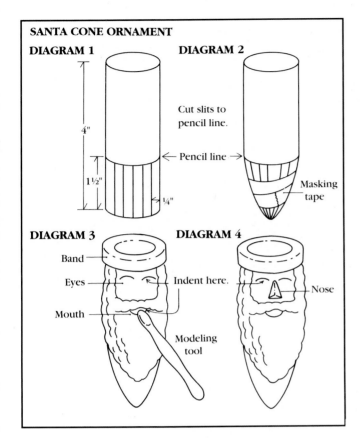

SANTA CONE ORNAMENT

DIAGRAM 1

4"

1½"

¼"

DIAGRAM 2

Cut slits to pencil line.

← Pencil line →

Masking tape

DIAGRAM 3

Band

Eyes

Mouth

Indent here.

Modeling tool

DIAGRAM 4

Nose

For hanger, cut a 10" length of twine, thread 1 end through each hole in cone, and tie knots large enough to keep twine from slipping through holes. Fill cone with dried moss and berries as desired.

Shell Santa Necklace

Materials:
oyster shell
electric drill with ¼" bit
papier mâché
modeling tool
texture paste
small paintbrush
ceramic paints: black, white, antique white, brick red
paint thinner
antiquing mud (also called art mud)
26" piece of satin cord

Note: Papier mâché takes at least 48 hours to dry and must be thoroughly dry before paint is applied. Texture paste and antiquing mud are available at local craft stores.

Using electric drill, drill a hole ¾" to 1" from narrow top edge of shell. (Placement may differ slightly depending on shell length.) Following manufacturer's instructions, prepare papier mâché. Referring to photograph, build hatband, mustache, and top of beard with papier mâché and modeling tool.

Apply a layer of papier mâché to build facial features. Referring to Diagram 3 of Santa Cone Ornament and using modeling tool, make shallow indentations for eyes and mouth. Referring to Diagram 4, shape nose by forming a small elongated triangle from remaining papier mâché and pressing it lightly onto middle of face, blending edges smoothly. Allow to dry.

When dry, coat entire surface with texture paste. Allow to dry. Referring to photograph, paint on features.

When paint is thoroughly dry, make a thin wash with equal parts paint thinner and antiquing mud and paint over entire front of shell. Wipe off excess. Allow to dry.

To finish necklace, fold cord in half. Insert folded end through hole in shell. Pull cut ends as 1 through loop and tie ends into a knot.

Can This Be Paper?

You'll be pleasantly surprised to find that the dramatic jewelry featured here is extremely easy to make, inexpensive, and lots of fun to wear.

Above: You can adapt the papier-mâché mixture to make accessories like the star pendant shown at left. Simply mix papier-mâché with craft glue instead of water until a dough-like consistency is formed. Roll the mixture out on waxed paper. Using a cookie cutter, cut out the desired shapes, trimming away the excess with a knife. Poke a hole through the top with a toothpick. Dry the pendant in the oven at 200° for about 10 minutes. After it dries, paint the pendant, decorate it as desired, and thread a ribbon through the hole.

Papier-mâché Pins

Line a metal candy mold with a piece of wet newspaper, one inch larger all around than the mold. Tamp the paper down into all crevices of the mold. Following manufacturer's instructions, mix the papier-mâché and press it into the lined mold. Bake the filled mold in the oven at 200° for 10 to 15 minutes, depending on the depth of the mold. Before the papier-mâché is completely dry, remove the mold from the oven and press the papier-mâché firmly down into the mold again, adding more if necessary to keep the back level. Remove the pin from the mold and return it to the oven until it is completely dry. Trim the ragged ends of the newspaper away from the edges of the pin.

Personalize the pin with acrylic paints and embellish it with assorted rhinestones, sequins, and trims secured with epoxy glue. Finish the pin by gluing a bar-pin accessory to the back.

Paper Beads

You can make beads and necklaces with a technique similar to old-time quilling. (Quilling is rolling thin strips of paper into designs and objects.)

Use medium-weight paper to make the beads. For seasonal jewelry, cut your strips from red and green paper and glue to a paper backing before cutting.

Refer to the Diagram to cut the paper for the long bead. For the shorter bead, the base of the triangle should be ⅜ inch. For the flat bead, cut a ¼- or ⅛-inch-wide paper strip with parallel edges, 4¼ inches in length.

To roll the beads, make a 1¼-inch slit in the unpointed end of a six-inch wooden skewer. Slide the wide end of a paper triangle into the slit and with your fingers, spread craft glue over the entire inside of the paper triangle and continue rolling until the bead is formed. Slip the bead off the skewer and dab away any excess glue.

To make earrings, string a ⅛-inch flat bead onto a 10-inch length of matching thread. Double the thread with the bead in the center and push the two ends of the thread through several more beads. Tie a knot to secure on the end of an earring hook and trim threads. For a necklace or bracelet, cut elasticized thread the desired length and then string beads and miniature jingle bells together, if desired, knotting ends of thread.

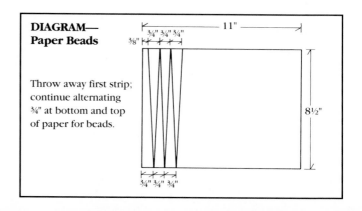

DIAGRAM—Paper Beads

¾" ¾" ¾" 11"

⅜"

Throw away first strip; continue alternating ¾" at bottom and top of paper for beads.

8½"

¾" ¾" ¾"

Above: Creativity is the main ingredient needed to hand-craft these paper jewels, which you can make with a few basic techniques. An array of acrylic paints and shiny baubles will lend personality.

Above: Because of the wide variety of colors and prints available, wrapping paper is an ideal medium to use to make seasonal jewelry. Glue wrapping paper to medium-weight paper with spray adhesive and then let it dry before cutting.

Right: Unable to find the right color combinations for your bead needs? Try sponge-painting the paper before cutting. This will allow you to combine several colors in an unusual speckled look. Just dip the edge of a sponge in acrylic paint, dab excess onto newspaper, and sponge colors in a design onto the paper. Then let the design dry.

Left: In their simple elegance, these ivory paper beads might be carved from wood.

Treasured Traditions

Borrowing from the Amish

All of these projects were inspired by the bold, bright colors found in Amish quilts and needlework.

Sunshine and Shadow Doll Quilt

Materials:
¾ yard (45"-wide) rust cotton
¼ yard (45"-wide) medium green cotton
¼ yard (45"-wide) robin's egg blue cotton
⅛ yard (45"-wide) each of cotton: maroon,
 spruce green, Christmas green, grass green,
 yellow-green, indigo, azure blue, sky blue,
 coral, pomegranate, Christmas red
24" square of thin quilt batting
threads to match fabrics

Note: Finished size is 24" square. Wash, dry, and press all fabrics. All seam allowances are ¼".

From rust fabric, cut 1 (25") square for backing. From medium green, cut 2 (2¾" x 19¼") strips and 2 (2¾" x 23¾") strips for outer border. From robin's egg blue, cut 2 (1¼" x 17¾") strips and 2 (1¼" x 19¼") strips for inner border, and 2 (1¼" x 45") strips. From maroon, cut 10 (1¼") squares and set aside for use in center diamond. From each of remaining fabrics, cut 2 (1¼" x 45") strips.

Referring to Diagram 1 for color placement, stitch 24 (1¼" x 45") strips together lengthwise. Press seam allowances to the left. Cut across joined strips at 1¼" intervals to make 23 strips, each with 24 pieced-square units. Position 23 strips side by side with colors aligned.

Referring to Diagram 2, Row 1, for position and using seam ripper, pick apart seams to remove 1 yellow-green square (reserve the square for another use).

Referring to Diagram 2, Row 2, for position, and using seam ripper, separate strip into 4 sections as shown. Reserve square marked R. Repeat to separate Rows 3-23 into sections as shown, removing and reserving squares marked R.

Using the 10 individual 1¼" maroon squares, plus reserved maroon, pomegranate, Christmas red, and coral squares, piece strips for center diamond (see Diagram 3).

Referring to Diagram 4 and working 1 row at a time, reposition pieced sections of Rows 2-22, moving outside units of each row to center of same row as shown. Sections in Rows 1 and 23 remain in same position. Add pieced strips for center diamond to centers of Rows 9-15 as shown.

Join sections in Row 1 to complete strip. Repeat for Rows 2-23.

Arrange the strips so that seams for odd-numbered rows are pressed to the left and seams for even-numbered rows are pressed to the right. Match seam lines (pin for best results) and join rows to complete pieced center.

For robin's egg blue inner borders, with right sides facing and raw edges aligned, stitch a 1¼" x 17¾" border strip to each side of quilt; then stitch a 1¼" x 19¼" strip to top and bottom edges in same manner. Press seams toward border.

For medium green outer borders, with right sides facing and raw edges aligned, stitch a 2¾" x 19¼" border strip to each side of quilt; then stitch a 2¾" x 23¾" strip to top and bottom edges in same manner. Press seams toward border.

Stack rust backing (right side down), batting, and pieced top (right side up). Working from center outward, baste through all layers to secure. Using matching threads, machine-stitch in-the-ditch along both sides of inner border and ⅜" inside raw outer edges.

Turn under ¼" along edges of backing, fold backing to front of quilt to make a ⅜" self-binding, and slipstitch folded edge of binding to front of quilt, covering machine-quilting stitches and mitering corners.

DIAGRAM 1—Basic Strip (Cut 23)

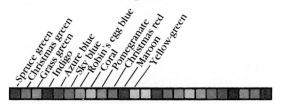

DIAGRAM 2—Dividing Strips into Sections

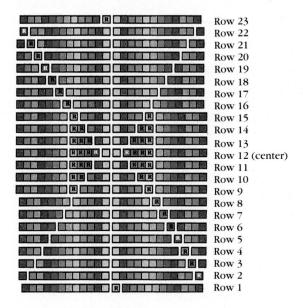

DIAGRAM 3—Strips for Center Diamond

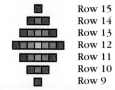

DIAGRAM 4—Repositioning Strips

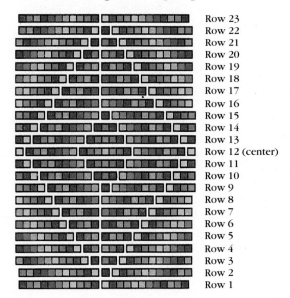

Vine Doll Bed

Materials:
4 (1½" x 1½" x 4¾") pieces of pine for legs
2 (2½" x 9") pieces of ¾"-thick pine for frame
2 (2½" x 19") pieces of ¾"-thick pine for frame
2 (¾" x 7½") pieces of ½"-thick pine for slat
    support
2 (¾" x 16") pieces of ½"-thick pine for slat
    support
5 (1¼" x 9") pieces of ¼"-thick pine for slats
sandpaper: 100 grit, 150 grit
coping saw
wood glue
#4 finishing nails
wire brad nails: #18 (1¼"), #19 (½")
½" tacks
walnut wood stain
2 (45"-long) pliable vines, about ½"-thick
8 (45"-long) pliable vines, about ¼"-thick
¾ yard (45"-wide) muslin
polyester stuffing

Note: Grape and kudzu vines are among the most adaptable for bending.

Before beginning construction of bed, sand all wood pieces, beginning with 100 grit sandpaper and finishing with 150 grit. Referring to Diagram 1, Figure A, divide 1 end of 1 leg piece into fourths by drawing cross shape. Then measure ¾" down from this end and mark around all 4 sides. With coping saw, cut away all but 1 of the quarters down to the ¾" mark. (This will leave 1 quarter standing to use as a peg. See Figure B.) Repeat on 3 remaining leg pieces.

To make bed frame, glue 9" and 19" frame pieces together, with 9" pieces between 19" pieces, to form a rectangle. Secure with finishing nails. Referring to Diagram 2 and with pegs inside corners of frame, glue legs to frame. Secure with 1¼" wire brad nails.

Referring to Diagram 3, glue 7½" pieces of slat support inside frame between pegs on legs. Using 1¼" wire brad nails, attach to frame. Repeat with 16" pieces of slat support on long sides of frame. Space 5 slats evenly on slat supports. Using ½" tacks, attach slats to slat supports.

Following manufacturer's instructions, apply walnut stain to all surfaces. Let dry.

For headboard, cut 1 (½") vine 42" long, making sure cut is straight. Make a straight cut on other end of vine. Bend vine into U shape. Referring to Diagram 4, line vine ends up with bottoms of 2 legs, and attach vine to bed frame on 9" end of frame with 1¼"

wire brad nails. Cut 1 (¼") vine approximately 3" shorter than first vine. Placing vine just inside first vine, follow same procedure for attaching to frame. Cut 2 (¼") vines 34" long. Leaving 8" on each end untwisted, twist center portion of 2 vines together. Following procedure for first and second vines, attach to frame. Weave 1 (¼") vine through headboard structure as shown in Diagram 4 to form heart shape. Using ½" wire brad nails, attach to frame and to other vines.

For footboard, follow same procedure as for headboard, cutting 1 (½") vine 35" long, 1 (¼") vine approximately 3" shorter, 2 (¼") twisted vines 25" long, and 1 (¼") heart vine 34" long.

For mattress, cut 2 (12" x 20") pieces of muslin. With right sides facing and using ½" seam allowances, stitch together, leaving 1 end open for stuffing. Turn. Stuff loosely with polyester stuffing. Whipstitch opening closed.

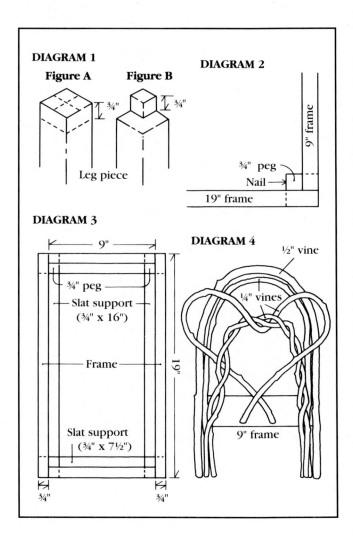

Crocheted Amish Balls

Materials for 1 ball:
1 (2½"-diameter) craft foam ball
black acrylic paint
paintbrush
size 5 pearl cotton: 1 (27-yard) skein each red, green, light green, hot pink, turquoise, fuchsia, blue, lavender, black
size B crochet hook

Note: Crochet Abbreviations are on page 153. Several ornaments can be made from the amount of thread listed above.

Paint craft foam ball black. Let dry.

TRIANGLE: *Rnd 1:* With red, ch 5 (counts as 1 dc and ch 2), dc in 5th ch from hook, ch 2, * dc in same ch as before, ch 2, rep from * 3 times more, sl st in 3rd ch of beg ch-5. *Rnd 2:* Ch 2, 2 sc in next ch-2 sp, ch 3, (3 sc in each of next 2 sps, ch 3) twice, 3 sc in next ch-2 sp, sl st in top of beg ch-2. *Rnd 3:* Ch 2, * sc in each sc to next ch-3 lp, (sc, ch 3, sc) in lp, rep from * around, sl st in top of beg ch-2. Fasten off.

Rep rnds 1-3 to make 1 triangle from each color except black.

ASSEMBLY: Hold any 2 triangles with wrong sides facing and edges aligned. Working through both pieces, join black in corner lp, sc in same lp, sc in each sc across to next corner lp. Do not fasten off. Pick up 2 more triangles and join them in same manner. (Work additional sc in corner lps as needed to keep work flat.) Continue in same manner until all triangles are joined to form a row of 4 diamonds. Fasten off.

Work in same manner to join edges of 3 diamonds. Insert painted ball in crocheted cover and join remaining edges in same manner. Do not fasten off.

To make hanger, ch 10 or desired length, sl st in last sc on ball to join.

Right: The brighter the better is the one rule to keep in mind when creating these Amish-inspired ornaments, which include Crocheted Amish Balls, Embroidered Felt Ornaments, Gleaming Ornaments, and tassels. The Amish Icicles are a snap to make. Transfer the pattern on page 149 to an aluminum sheet, paint the entire surface with markers, and then cut out as indicated to create the spiral.

Amish Colors

Decorating a tree is not part of the Amish Christmas; however, the crafters of the ornaments below could not resist the daring color combinations of Amish crafts.

The Amish project their life-style of humility and hard work into their decorative crafts; the result is a distinctive textile art form that is marked by striking contrasts. Their work ethic can be seen in the meticulous quilting of Amish quilts and the attention to detail in Amish needlework samplers.

Amish women often have colorful flower gardens, which they see as arrangements of nature's beauty. These natural colors, along with the dark basic colors of Amish dress, form the palette of their textile arts. Patterned fabrics, seen as worldly and prideful, are never used. Instead, the effects of contrast and shading are created through the manipulation of solid colors. Traditional Amish artists favor deep colors positioned against bright blues and greens.

Embroidered Felt Ornament

Materials for 1 ornament:
pattern on page 149
scraps of black or red felt
1 (2½"-diameter) craft foam ball
straight pins
size 5 pearl cotton: green, light green, hot pink, red, lavender, blue, turquoise, black, fuchsia
crewel needle
tassel to coordinate with ball (instructions on page 65)

Transfer pattern to felt and cut 6.

Stretch felt pieces over foam ball so that tips meet at top and bottom of ball and sides slightly overlap. Secure with straight pins.

Using 1 strand of matching pearl cotton, whipstitch tips of opposite felt pieces together at top of ball. Repeat at bottom of ball. Do not stitch along side seams.

For hanger, stitch a 6" piece of pearl cotton through top center of ornament and knot ends.

Referring to Diagram 1 and using desired color, feather-stitch overlapped sides of felt pieces together along first, third, and fifth seam lines.

Referring to Diagram 2 and using desired color, double feather-stitch overlapped sides of felt pieces together along remaining seam lines.

Referring to Diagram 3 and using desired colors, embellish feather stitches by embroidering French knots and additional stitching.

Tack tassel to bottom of ball.

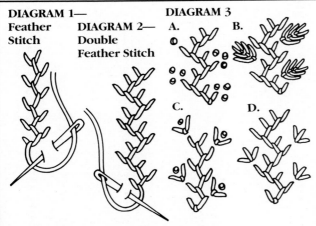

DIAGRAM 1—Feather Stitch

DIAGRAM 2—Double Feather Stitch

DIAGRAM 3
A. B. C. D.

A. Double feather stitch with French knots
B. Double feather stitch with 3-layered fly stitches
C. Single feather stitches with French knots
D. Single feather stitches with fly stitch and straight stitch

Gleaming Ornaments

Materials:
patterns on page 149
graphite paper
cardstock paper (80# weight)
aluminum sheet (large disposable oven liner)
old washcloth
felt-tip permanent markers: jewel tones
nail or ice pick
monofilament
thin silver cord
small jingle bell
1 medium and 2 small tassels (instructions on page 65)

Using graphite paper, transfer pattern and markings to cardstock paper. Cut out pattern to use as a template. With scissors, cut off and discard sides of pan. Tape template to aluminum sheet and cut out. With template still in place, place face up on dry washcloth. Using dull pencil, trace diamonds and design lines on templates, pressing hard enough to score (but not cut through) aluminum.

Remove template and turn piece face down on washcloth. Retrace diamonds and design lines with pencil. (This will reverse the previous indentations.) Referring to photograph and using pencil, make stipple marks over entire surface, except within design areas.

Still working on washcloth and back of ornament, use pencil to indent diamonds (and raise them on front of ornament) by pressing firmly within outlines in a back and forth motion. To bevel edges of small star, with star face down on washcloth, trace just inside outer edge with pencil. Move ornament to a hard work surface (still face down). Using motions described above, again rub diamonds with pencil to smooth surface.

Turn ornament face up. Outline small star and color in diamonds with markers. Using nail or ice pick, punch holes as indicated on pattern. For moon ornament, attach bell with silver cord and star with monofilament through holes. For diamond ornament, attach 2 small tassels to side corners and 1 medium tassel to bottom corner of diamond. Thread silver cord through top hole for hanger.

Tassel with Paper Bead

Materials for 1 tassel:
2 (1" x 22½") strips of newspaper
craft glue
size 5 pearl cotton in 3 colors of choice
4" square of cardboard
darning needle
felt-tip markers to match pearl cotton
embroidery scissors

To make paper bead, wrap end of 1 newspaper strip once around a pencil; glue and continue rolling tightly around pencil. Glue end of strip to secure. Glue end of second strip to rolled piece; roll tightly around first roll and glue end to roll. Let dry; then remove paper bead from pencil.

Referring to photograph, choose a different color of pearl cotton for tassel body, to cover bead, and for accent bands.

To make tassel body, lay 1 pearl cotton thread across cardboard, leaving a 1" tail. Hold thread in place and wrap around cardboard 40 times. Cut last thread to same length as tail piece. For hanger, thread needle with 8" strand of matching pearl cotton. Slide needle under end of bundle opposite tail pieces (see Diagram 1). Tie strand in a very tight knot around bundle. Cut bundle end opposite hanger, remove cardboard, and smooth tassel with fingers. Trim ends even.

Use marker to color paper bead to match the thread that will cover it. Thread needle with 3 yards of thread, pulling ends even. Insert needle between paper layers, pulling through so that ends of thread are hidden. To cover bead, wrap thread through hole in bead and continue wrapping bead lengthwise, pulling with even tension and keeping threads smooth and parallel. To secure thread, push needle through paper layers again, pulling tightly. Clip thread close to bead.

Left: Use the tassel instructions below to create these earrings. From a pair of purchased metal button forms, remove the wire button shanks with pliers. Following manufacturer's instructions, cover the button forms with fabric. If desired, crisscross pearl cotton across the top of the buttons. Hot-glue earring posts or clips to the button backs and tack small tassels to the base of the finished earrings.

Pull top of tassel body through center of bead so that ½" of tassel top extends above top of bead.

To make accent bands, thread needle with a 24" length of contrasting thread and push it down through hole from top of bead to bottom (see Diagram 2). Leave tail of thread hidden inside bead. Wrap thread tightly around tassel at base of bead until thread band is ¼"-wide. Insert needle under bottom of thread band and into hole of bead to top of bead (see Diagram 3). Wrap thread tightly around tassel at top of bead to make a band ¼"-wide. Insert needle under top thread band and push down through hole to base of bead. Clip thread close to bead. Trim ends of tassel even, if necessary.

Banded tassel: Referring to photographs on pages 59 and 63, choose a different color of pearl cotton for tassel body, accent band, and contrasting accent bands.

To make tassel body, follow instructions for tassel with paper bead, substituting a 3" square of cardboard and wrapping thread 30 times.

To make center accent band, thread needle with a 12" length of thread. Beginning ½" from tassel top, hold thread tail and wrap thread tightly over tail and around tassel. Continue until band is ¼"-wide. Insert needle under band and push up from bottom to top. Clip both ends of thread close to band.

To make contrasting accent bands, refer to instructions for accent bands on tassel with paper bead, making bands ⅛"-wide instead of ¼"-wide.

Small tassel: Refer to instructions for banded tassel, substituting a 2" square of cardboard and wrapping thread 25 times.

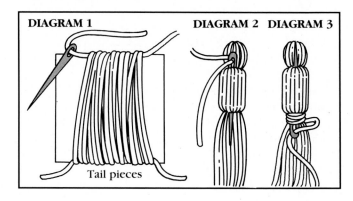

DIAGRAM 1   **DIAGRAM 2 DIAGRAM 3**

Tail pieces

65

Chestnuts—
Roasting, Baking, and Broiling—
on an Open Fire

The poulterers' shops were still half open, and the fruiterers' were radiant in their glory. There were great round, pot-bellied baskets of chestnuts, shaped like the waistcoats of jolly old gentlemen, lolling at the doors, and tumbling out into the street in their apoplectic opulence.

—Charles Dickens, A Christmas Carol

Since the first Thanksgiving feast, when American Indians shared them with settlers, chestnuts have been a part of the festive season. Street vendors in Chicago, New York, and Philadelphia carry on the tradition by roasting chestnuts on busy street corners for holiday shoppers.

Now you can share the traditional chestnut with family and friends with recipes like Cream of Chestnut Soup, Mushroom and Chestnut Stuffing, and Orange Chestnut Broccoli.

White-Chocolate Chestnut Charlotte

1½ cups shelled chestnuts
18 ladyfingers, split lengthwise
4 ounces white chocolate, grated
1½ cups whipping cream, divided
4 eggs, separated
½ cup sugar, divided
2 teaspoons unflavored gelatin
¼ cup cold water
2 tablespoons Grand Marnier or other orange-
   flavored liqueur
Whipped cream
White chocolate curls
Fresh strawberries

Position knife blade in food processor bowl; add chestnuts. Cover and process until chestnuts are coarsely ground; set aside.

Line bottom and sides of a 9" springform pan with ladyfingers; set aside.

Combine white chocolate and ¼ cup whipping cream in top of a double boiler; bring water to a boil. Reduce heat to low; cook until chocolate melts, stirring occasionally. Remove from heat; cool to room temperature.

Beat remaining 1¼ cups whipping cream in a medium bowl until soft peaks form; cover and chill.

Beat egg yolks in a large mixing bowl until thick and lemon-colored (about 5 minutes). Gradually add ¼ cup sugar, 1 tablespoon at a time, beating until smooth. Fold in white chocolate mixture; set aside.

Sprinkle gelatin over cold water in a small saucepan; let stand 1 minute. Cook over low heat until gelatin dissolves; cool slightly. Fold gelatin mixture and Grand Marnier into yolk mixture; set aside.

Beat egg whites (at room temperature), until soft peaks form. Gradually add remaining ¼ cup sugar, 1 tablespoon at a time, beating until stiff peaks form.

Gently fold ground chestnuts, beaten egg white mixture, and chilled whipped cream into yolk mixture. Spoon into prepared springform pan; cover and chill 8 hours.

To serve, carefully remove sides of springform pan. Garnish with whipped cream, white chocolate curls, and strawberries. Yield: 10 to 12 servings.

Above: This creamy chocolaty charlotte has an unexpected mellow chestnut flavor, as well as a dash of Grand Marnier.

Choosing Chestnuts

Fresh chestnuts are available at farmers' markets, produce stands, and oriental markets in November and December. Though primarily grown in Italy, chestnuts are also cultivated in France, Spain, China, the United States, and the Dominican Republic. In the States, blight-resistant varieties can be produced in any peach-growing region of the country.

Choose plump, shiny, firm chestnuts. They should be heavy for their size and free of blemishes. Also examine nuts carefully for spoilage. (Spoilage is common since chestnuts don't keep well.) Ask to examine the inside of a few chestnuts. The meat should be white and firm.

To prepare chestnuts for shelling and cooking, the shell of each chestnut must be broken or pierced enough to allow for expansion while cooking. To do this, place a chestnut on a chopping block, flat side up, and hit it with a hammer or meat mallet.

To roast and shell chestnuts, place up to one pound of prepared nuts in a single layer in a shallow roasting pan. Bake at 400° for 15 minutes. Let chestnuts cool just enough to handle and then shell.

To microwave and shell chestnuts, place 10 prepared chestnuts in a circular pattern on a small plate. Microwave at HIGH 1½ minutes.

Let chestnuts cool just enough to handle.

Of course, chestnuts can be roasted over an open fire. Place prepared chestnuts in a wire basket, a perforated chestnut pan, a large skillet, or an open-fire popcorn popper. Cook over an open fire, shaking pan frequently, until chestnuts are lightly charred.

Chestnuts are also available already shelled. For information about ordering chestnuts, see the source listing on page 154.

Cream of Chestnut Soup

1 medium leek
2 carrots, scraped and shredded
1 clove garlic, minced
2 tablespoons butter or margarine
3 cups canned diluted chicken broth
2 cups shelled, coarsely chopped chestnuts,
    toasted
1 bay leaf
1 cup milk
1 cup whipping cream
2 tablespoons dry sherry
½ teaspoon salt
⅛ teaspoon ground white pepper
Leek slices (optional)

Remove root, tough outer leaves, and top from leek, leaving 2" of dark leaves. Wash leek and thinly slice.

Sauté leek, carrots, and garlic in butter in a Dutch oven until tender. Add chicken broth, chestnuts, and bay leaf. Cook, uncovered, over medium heat 25 minutes or until vegetables are tender. Remove and discard bay leaf.

Transfer chestnut mixture in batches to container of an electric blender; process until smooth. Return chestnut mixture to Dutch oven. Stir in milk and next 4 ingredients. Cook over low heat until thoroughly heated. Garnish each serving with leek slices, if desired. Yield: 8 cups.

Note: Soup may also be served chilled.

Chestnut Scones

2 cups all-purpose flour
3 tablespoons sugar
2 teaspoons baking powder
½ teaspoon baking soda
¼ teaspoon salt
⅓ cup butter or margarine
½ cup sour cream
1 egg, lightly beaten
⅔ cup shelled, finely chopped chestnuts,
    toasted
2 tablespoons apple jelly, melted

Combine all-purpose flour, sugar, baking powder, baking soda, and salt in a medium bowl; stir well. Cut in butter with a pastry blender until mixture resembles coarse meal. Add sour cream and egg,

Above: Begin any winter meal with a steaming bowl of rich Cream of Chestnut Soup, and your guests will remember a feast.

stirring just until dry ingredients are moistened. Stir in chestnuts.

Turn dough out onto a lightly floured surface and knead 4 or 5 times. Pat dough into an 8" circle on a greased baking sheet. Cut circle into 8 wedges, using a sharp knife; separate wedges slightly. Bake at 400° for 15 minutes or until lightly browned. Brush with melted apple jelly and serve warm. Yield: 8 scones.

Vanilla Chestnut Soufflé

1 (6") vanilla bean
2 tablespoons butter or margarine
¼ cup all-purpose flour
¾ cup milk
⅔ cup sugar, divided
4 eggs, separated
¾ cup shelled, finely chopped chestnuts,
    toasted
Rich Caramel Sauce (recipe follows)

Cut a piece of aluminum foil long enough to circle a 1½-quart soufflé dish, plus a 1" overlap. Fold foil lengthwise into thirds. Lightly butter 1 side of foil and bottom of dish. Wrap foil around top, buttered side to dish, so that foil extends 3" above rim. Secure with string and set aside.

Split vanilla bean in half lengthwise; scrape vanilla seeds from bean; set aside. Melt butter in a medium saucepan over low heat; add flour, stirring until smooth. Cook for 1 minute, stirring constantly. Gradually add milk and ⅓ cup sugar; cook over medium heat, stirring constantly, until mixture is

thickened and bubbly. Stir in reserved vanilla seeds.

Beat egg yolks in a mixing bowl until thick and lemon-colored (about 5 minutes). Gradually stir about ¼ of hot mixture into yolks; add to remaining hot mixture, stirring constantly. Set aside.

Beat egg whites (at room temperature) until soft peaks form. Gradually add remaining ⅓ cup sugar, 1 tablespoon at a time, beating until stiff peaks form. Fold egg whites and chestnuts into yolk mixture. Spoon mixture into prepared soufflé dish.

Bake at 475° for 10 minutes; reduce temperature to 400° and bake an additional 15 minutes or until golden brown. Remove aluminum collar and serve immediately with Rich Caramel Sauce. Yield: 8 servings.

Rich Caramel Sauce:

1 cup sugar
½ cup butter
½ cup whipping cream

Sprinkle sugar in a heavy skillet; place over medium heat. Cook, stirring constantly, until sugar melts and syrup is light golden brown. Remove from heat; add butter and stir until melted.

Return mixture to low heat; gradually add whipping cream, 1 tablespoon at a time, stirring constantly. Continue to cook over low heat, stirring constantly, 10 minutes or until mixture is thickened and creamy. Remove from heat and cool slightly. Yield: 1 cup.

Mushroom and Chestnut Stuffing

½ pound mushrooms, sliced
1 medium onion, chopped
2 stalks celery, chopped
1 clove garlic, minced
2 tablespoons butter or margarine, melted
1 teaspoon rubbed sage
½ teaspoon dried whole thyme
½ teaspoon salt
½ teaspoon pepper
½ pound bulk pork sausage, cooked and crumbled
1 cup shelled, coarsely chopped chestnuts, toasted
2 cups cornbread crumbs
1 cup soft bread crumbs
¾ cup canned chicken broth, undiluted
2 teaspoons butter or margarine

Sauté mushrooms, onion, celery, and garlic in butter in a large skillet until tender. Stir in sage, thyme, salt, and pepper.

Combine mushroom mixture, sausage, chestnuts, cornbread crumbs, and soft bread crumbs in a large bowl; stir well. Add chicken broth, stirring well. Spoon mixture into a 13" x 9" x 2" baking dish. Dot with butter.

Bake at 325° for 20 to 25 minutes or until lightly browned. Yield: 8 servings.

Orange Chestnut Broccoli

1 large orange
1¼ cups shelled, coarsely chopped chestnuts
1 shallot, sliced
2 teaspoons butter or margarine, melted
2 teaspoons vegetable oil
2¼ cups orange juice
1½ cups water
¼ cup plus 2 tablespoons firmly packed brown sugar
1½ teaspoons beef-flavored bouillon granules
¼ teaspoon pepper
1 pound broccoli
1 tablespoon water
2 teaspoons cornstarch

Peel orange, removing white pith. Slice orange into ¼" slices; set aside.

Sauté chestnuts and shallot in butter and oil in a large skillet until chestnuts are lightly browned. Combine orange juice, water, brown sugar, bouillon granules, and pepper; add to chestnut mixture. Bring to a boil; reduce heat and simmer, uncovered, 25 minutes.

Trim off large leaves of broccoli and remove tough ends of lower stalks. Wash broccoli thoroughly and cut into spears. Arrange broccoli in vegetable steamer over boiling water. Cover and steam 5 to 8 minutes or until crisp-tender.

Combine water and cornstarch; stir well. Add to chestnut mixture and cook over medium heat, stirring constantly, until mixture is thickened and bubbly.

Arrange broccoli and reserved orange slices on a serving platter. Top with chestnut mixture. Yield: 6 servings.

Giving in Style

For many families, Christmas has become a blur of shopping—a trudge from one store to the next in endless traffic. But not for the Ganchan family of Houston, Texas. Mildred and Dick Ganchan have a son, Richard, and three daughters, Kenzie, Meg, and Susan, all with families of their own.

The Ganchans decided nearly 25 years ago that they wanted to capture the real spirit of Christmas during the holiday. When their daughters were in high school, Mildred and Dick hit on an idea that has become a very special tradition.

"We decided to draw names," Mildred explains. After opening gifts on Christmas night, the family draws one name each for the next year.

What's so special about drawing names? Well, the Ganchans add a twist of creativity. Each family member plans a unique presentation to accompany a gift, which is often handmade—a crocheted afghan or a hand-sewn bathrobe from Mildred, for example. In such a fun-loving and talented family as the Ganchan clan, each gift introduction leads to theatrics, song, or poetry.

"We either do a skit or write a poem or sing a song. Some are wonderful, but, of course, some are not," she laughs. "We get better with age!"

According to daughter Susan, the gifts are almost irrelevant. "It's the presentation that really counts," she says. "We're kind of a show-business type of family." She admits what might be expected—a healthy sibling rivalry exists: "Of course, we always try to outdo one another!"

With expectations and good-humored competition at fever pitch, each family member listens carefully all year for that perfect unsuspected hint.

"I drew Dad's name one year and I thought, 'What am I going to get him? He's got everything he wants,'" Susan remembers worrying. She needn't have. The much-needed clue was dropped at a family birthday party when her father lamented, "I'm the only one in the family who doesn't have a Christmas stocking." That Christmas he received a handmade red satin stocking—in the shape of a Texas cowboy boot.

Last year, Meg organized a box of family photographs—collected over the last 50 years—into five huge albums for her mother's present. "But first she read me the sweetest, dearest poem," Mildred remembers.

The youngest of 10 grandchildren, John, age

Above: On Christmas night, the Ganchan clan, all dressed for the festivities, gathers at the family retreat, the Browning Plantation.

seven, *sang* his presentation last year. A few years before this, Kenzie's husband, David, got in on the singing. He gave Mildred an answering machine, and then sang "I Just Called To Say I Love You."

In 1983, to help the holiday mood even further, the Ganchans bought and finely restored an antebellum

70

Left: Presents given over the years include a red satin cowboy-boot stocking that Susan made for her father, an apron for Mildred decorated with the green handprints of all her grandchildren, photographs (framed by son-in-law Steve) of Dick as a flight instructor in World War II, and a picture of Susan's home, painted by her aunt.

71

house located about an hour from Houston. The Browning Plantation, now listed in the National Register of Historic Places, has become a charming bed-and-breakfast, an elegant meeting place for area clubs and tours, and—most especially—a family retreat. During the holidays, the rafters ring with the family's songs and antics.

Even though they work hard on each of their special presentations, family members never forget others—especially those in need—during the holidays. They choose a family that needs extra help and pitch in to buy them lots of presents.

The world may hustle and bustle more than ever these days. But after 25 years, this family's tradition seems to work fine. Each Ganchan focuses on presenting just one gift . . . and lots of love.

Above: This three-story Greek Revival mansion was built in the 1850s of cedar lumber hewn from trees on the property.

Below: The first year the Ganchan family celebrated Christmas at the plantation, Kenzie and Meg decorated every mantel and every room. When tour groups came through and saw the holiday handiwork, requests poured in for the sisters to share their talents. They now have their own Christmas decorating business, appropriately known as Elfin Glitz, since, imitating Santa's helpers, the two frequently dress in elf costumes as they decorate private homes and country clubs.

Above: Kenzie, Meg, and Susan look through an old photograph album they put together for their mother one Christmas when she was recovering from open-heart surgery. They selected some of her favorite photographed memories— her wedding portrait and pictures of her parents—to preserve in the antique velvet album.

Framed Keepsake Reindeer

A silhouette cut from artists' paper is an unusual way to frame a cherished patchwork piece or a favorite purchased print. If the fabric piece you choose to frame is a treasured heirloom, protect it by using acid-free or neutralized mat board, paper, and tape.

Materials:
pattern on page 150
tracing paper
11" x 14" piece of heavy-weight artists' paper
   for reindeer silhouette
craft knife
12" x 15" patchwork fabric (quilted or
   unquilted)
11" x 14" piece of heavy cardboard for backing
masking tape
11" x 14" piece of mat board
13" x 16" piece of cotton print to cover mat
   board
craft glue
11" x 14" purchased frame

Using tracing paper, center and transfer pattern to artists' paper and cut out with craft knife.

For backing, stretch patchwork fabric right side up over cardboard. Fold excess to back and secure with masking tape.

Center and cut a 7" x 10" window in mat board.

To cover mat board with fabric, place print fabric right side down on cutting surface. Apply glue thinly and evenly to 1 side of mat. Center and glue mat to wrong side of fabric, pressing down evenly. Draw a window on wrong side of fabric, 1" smaller than mat board window, and cut out. Clip fabric diagonally from inner window corners to corners of mat board. Bring excess fabric at top and bottom of window to back of mat and tape. Repeat for sides of window and outer edges of mat, easing at corners.

Stack patchwork-covered cardboard, cutout reindeer mat, and fabric-covered window mat. Place in frame.

Add your name and date to back of frame. If patchwork piece was handmade rather than purchased, note the maker's name and approximate date on back, also.

A Jolly Old Kansas Tearoom

An invitation to tea is a custom that speaks of friendship spirited by lively conversation, comforting foods, and a drink that warms the heart.

Above: Special holiday teatime recipes include scones with candied cherries, peppermint tea cake, and raspberry tea. Below: The Emerys' son, Robbie, helps wherever he can after school. Since he and his sister, Michelle, are out of school for Christmas holidays, they are often seen filling water glasses, setting the tables, and lighting candles in preparation for the big rush of visitors.

By the time Connie and Mike Emery happened on the for-sale sign, Haderway House was considered an eyesore. Built in 1900, the old farmhouse, a landmark of Lancaster, Kansas, had been vacant for seven years. But to Connie it was a dream come true. "Since I was four years old, I have dreamed of living in an old house," Connie says.

Influenced by her English grandfather, who celebrated teatime every day, Connie has always been fascinated by things British. Her grandparents cherished everything from their native country and surrounded themselves with antique furniture, fine linens, and china.

Connie's dream took form as renovation began on the Haderway House. Curious strangers poured in to see the development, and Mike kindly stopped work on the renovation to show them around. Connie was running a small bakery at the time and came across a box of old family recipes, including lemon tea bread and her grandmother's scones. It seemed that all the arrows were pointing in one direction: An English tearoom was born.

"I had antique silver, china, and linens," Connie says. "Since we hadn't finished the restoration, we were able to finish one room for the teahouse kitchen."

Open now for two years, the Haderway House tearoom has had visitors from 33 foreign countries and all 50 states. Visitors come for lunch, afternoon tea, and dinner, enjoying tea foods lovingly prepared by Connie.

At Christmastime, guests step in for a delightful experience. A warming fire glows in the fireplace, a pianist tickles carols from the grand piano in the parlor, and a luscious aroma of fudge and sugar cookies pours from the kitchen.

"My husband says that I'm a big kid at Christmas, and it *is* my favorite holiday of the year," admits Connie, who decorates the Haderway House with 15

silk trees. "Although visitors enjoy all my Victorian-style decorations, I decorate for me!"

It takes Connie and a friend two weeks to dress the Victorian house in its holiday finery. She uses silk greenery indoors so that the trees and garlands will last through the extended season, which continues through the week after Christmas—often the busiest time for the Emerys.

From eyesore to English teahouse, the Haderway House in the hands of the Emerys has made many dreams come true.

Above: In the family parlor, Connie and her daughter, Michelle, take time out for tea during their busy holiday schedule. Guests begin making reservations for the Christmas-season teas a year in advance. (For information about the Haderway House teahouse and tours, see the source listing on page 154.)

Right: An artificial garland, made elegant with gold lamé ribbon, Christmas balls, and baby's breath, curls down one leg of the grand piano. The garland is anchored at the top by a gold angel and at the bottom by a violin.

Above: The joint antique feather tree collection of Nancy Messinger and Sandra Pape was the beginning of their business together. This sampling of their collection includes two eight-inch-tall china-based feather trees with white paper flowers, tiny one-inch beige and white trees in the foreground, and a rare blue example with white berries.

Trees of a Feather

In Germany, the evergreen tree has always been the center of the Christmas festival. As early as 1605 in Strassburg, live fir trees were brought inside and decorated with wafers, sweets, gold foil, and apples. The tradition grew so quickly that by the 1800s it was not a luxury to have a tree at Christmas, but a necessity. Soon it was evident that German forests were being depleted by the popularity of this custom.

This may have been the time when the idea for an artificial alternative arose. There was no such thing as plastic, of course, but materials at hand were used. Thus, the goose-feather tree was created.

That's one theory of the feather tree's beginning. Another possibility is that the glass-ornament makers of Lauscha, Germany, made these spindly trees to use in displaying their wares throughout the year.

If their exact origin is unknown, what is plain is that these delicate little tabletop-size trees became heirloom treasures in the homes that adopted them. When German immigrants brought their prized possessions by boat to the New World, feather trees could be found folded up in their steamer trunks.

Once in America, the feather trees quickly became popular and began to appear in homes across the country. As the demand for the feather trees grew, more were imported from Germany—as were many of the blown-glass ornaments that were so nicely displayed on the trees. Mail-order houses such as Sears, Roebuck and Montgomery Ward offered the trees for sale throughout the 1920s and 1930s.

During this evolution of popularity, the feather tree continued to be built in the same way. Goose—and more rarely, turkey or ostrich—feathers were dyed green and then stripped from their quills. The feathers were wrapped around a sturdy wire. Numerous feathered branches were inserted into holes in a central wooden pole, which was then placed in a painted base.

The feather trees were seldom over 24 inches in height, allowing them to be displayed prominently on a table. Lots of small presents were tied onto the tree for decorations. Candy containers were also used to hold lightweight treats. Gilded fruits and nuts sparkled on the thin branches. Larger presents were displayed around the tree and sometimes a low wooden fence encircled the base.

The Tradition Lives On

About eight years ago, friends Nancy Messinger and Sandra Pape of Cedarburg, Wisconsin, began to evaluate their collection of antique feather trees. They had an impressive assortment, but it was getting harder and harder to find additional trees. Never ones to be discouraged, Sandra and Nancy decided they would just have to make their own.

"At first, we did a great deal of research," Nancy admits. They interviewed other collectors around the country and took a trip to a feather warehouse in Chicago.

Finally, they decided to get some hands-on experience. They bought chicken feathers from a nearby farm. After washing and then drying them in the dryer, they soon realized that chicken feathers were not for them. The soft white feathers

Above: Since Nancy, seated, and Sandra couldn't find a ready supply of feather trees to buy, they decided to make their own.

flew everywhere!

Now Nancy has her own business, Primitive Trees, Inc., a national company that makes feather trees.

For information about ordering hand-made feather trees, see the source listing on page 154.

Left: This antique feather tree in a window at Sandra Pape's home in Cedarburg, Wisconsin, shows how beautifully small antique glass ornaments can be displayed on the sparse branches.

Below: To find a feather tree on a musical stand is rare indeed. This one belongs to collector Jane Frank of St. Charles, Missouri. With a twist of the key, the music pours forth and the tree slowly turns.

After World War II, many feather trees were thrown out, since their German origin reminded Americans of the nation we had fought in the war. Those who could not bear to discard them hid them in attics, whence they were recovered in later years.

According to feather tree collector and Christmas book author Robert Brenner, feather trees now can be found from Los Angeles to Milwaukee to Santa Fe. "Anyone who sees the pictures of Christmas long ago," Robert says, "wants to explore that era. Anyone who has a respect for the past will appreciate the feather tree."

Recording the Holidays

If a picture is worth a thousand words, these clever methods for displaying your own photographs will certainly give you and your guests something to talk about!

Above: Covered in Christmassy print, this album makes a thoughtful gift or colorful accent for your tabletop.

Photograph Album

Capture memories from yesterday's pleasures in this album constructed from foam core covered with seasonal fabric. (For the filler pages, see the source listing on page 154.) Cut two pieces of foam core the same height as, and one inch wider than, the filler pages. Using adhesive spray, bond fabric to one side of each piece of foam core, overlapping and gluing edges to the inside of the album covers.

For the front cover, place one piece with fabric side down. With the right edges aligned, place one filler page on the cover front. Where the filler page bends, make a mark at the top and bottom of the cover. Remove the filler page and draw a line on the cover between the two marks. Lightly score the inside of the album cover along this line. (The cut will extend into the fabric overlap, *almost* to the very edge. You may need to score lightly several times to make the cover bend at this point.) For the linings, glue matching fabric, paper, or filler pages to the inside of the cover front and back. Using a hole punch, punch holes through the album covers to correspond with the filler pages, add filler pages, thread a 40-inch length of one-inch-wide ribbon through the holes, and tie a bow.

Portfolio

Exhibit favorite Christmas photographs in this stunning handmade portfolio. Refer to the photograph to construct this project. (Instructions are for the portfolio with the single ribbon.) Using adhesive spray, bond decorated paper to one side of a 16½ x 20-inch sheet of decorative mat board. Cut into six (10" x 5½") pieces.

To join pieces, lay them in a row, paper-side up and end to end, ⅛-inch apart. On the first piece on the left, center a small mark 2½ inches from the right end. Cut 3⅞ yards of 1½-inch-wide ribbon. Leaving 25 inches of ribbon on each end for ties, begin at mark and glue the ribbon along the center of each piece, using craft glue. Let the glue dry.

Turn the portfolio over. Using photo mounting corners, center and mount the photographs.

You can stretch the portfolio across your mantel to showcase your pictures, or simply fold it up with the photographs facing and secure with a bow (see top photograph on next page).

Right: You can display holiday pictures in one of these easy portfolios. To make the one standing up, simply use two ribbons for ties instead of one.

Right: Here's a handy and attractive way to organize all of those snapshots scattered in drawers and stashed in boxes: a shoebox and lid neatly covered in decorative paper. Dividers are used to organize photos into categories for easy reference.

Left: The wonderful thing about using pictures as ornaments is that no two are alike! Hot-glue red ribbon to the back of purchased frames to decorate a small tabletop tree with your favorite holiday photographs.

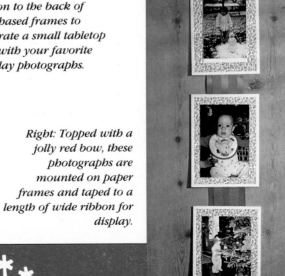

Right: Topped with a jolly red bow, these photographs are mounted on paper frames and taped to a length of wide ribbon for display.

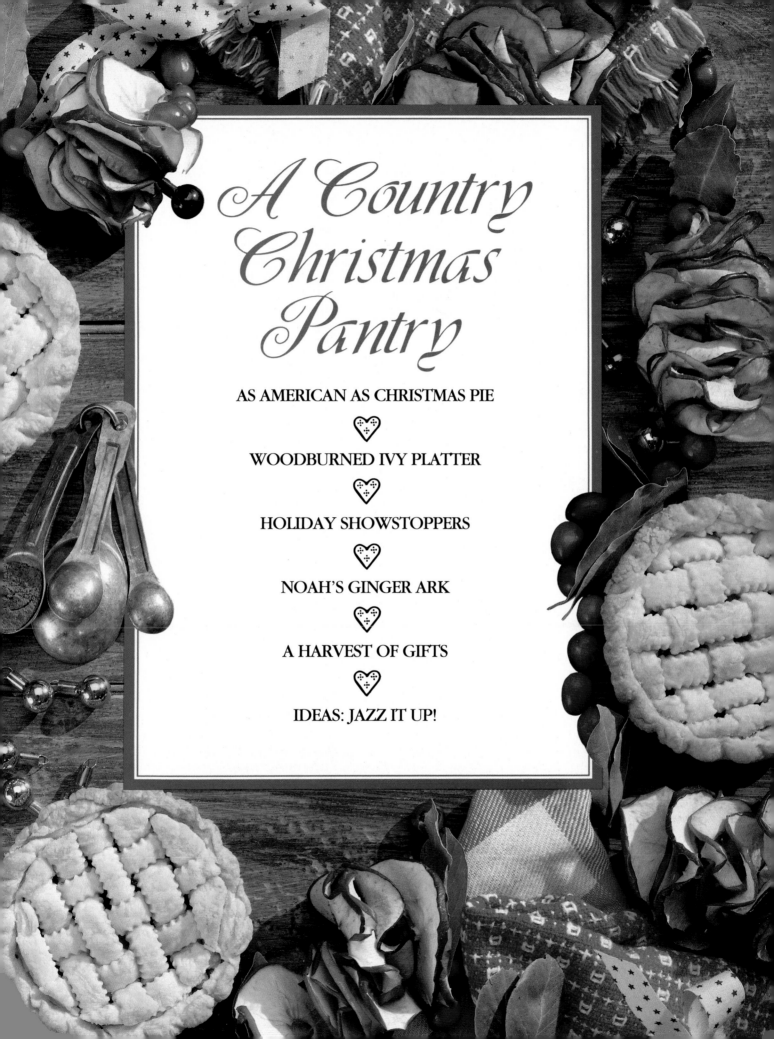

A Country Christmas Pantry

AS AMERICAN AS CHRISTMAS PIE

As American as Christmas Pie

At Christmastime, tradition is essential, but making something new and different can also be important. Here are some recipes that give traditional holiday pies and tarts a new twist. Choose from eight pie fillings, including Chocolate-Date Walnut and Lemon Slice Custard. These delicious fillings pair well with any of the five pastry variations.

Try the Double-Crust Cheddar Pastry with the Praline-Topped Pear Pie. For another tasty match, line tart tins with Toasted Nut Pastry and fill with Apricot Cheese.

Rum Raisin Apple Tarts

⅓ cup raisins
¼ cup dark rum
Pastry for 2 double-crust 9" pies
3 cups peeled, sliced cooking apples
1½ teaspoons lemon juice
¼ cup sugar
¼ cup firmly packed brown sugar
2 tablespoons all-purpose flour
¼ teaspoon ground cinnamon
¼ teaspoon ground nutmeg
1 tablespoon butter or margarine

Combine raisins and rum in a small bowl; cover and let stand 8 hours.

Roll half of pastry to ⅛" thickness on a lightly floured surface. Cut into 6" circles and place in 6 (4") tart pans with removable sides.

Combine apples and lemon juice in a large bowl; set aside. Combine sugars, flour, cinnamon, and nutmeg, mixing well. Spoon over apple mixture, tossing gently. Drain raisins, discarding rum. Add raisins to apple mixture; toss well. Spoon filling evenly into tart shells, and dot with butter.

Line large baking sheet with parchment paper; set aside. Roll remaining half of pastry to ⅛" thickness on a lightly floured surface; cut into ½" strips. Arrange strips in a tight weave, lattice fashion, on prepared baking sheet. Chill 1 hour. Cut into 6 (5") circles and carefully place 1 on each tart. Trim pastry even with edges of pans, fold edges under, and flute.

Bake at 450° for 10 minutes. Reduce heat to 350° and bake an additional 10 minutes or until golden brown. Cool completely. Yield: 6 (4") tarts.

Chocolate-Date Walnut Pie

Pastry for double-crust 9" pie
¾ cup light corn syrup
4 eggs
2 teaspoons vanilla extract
1 cup firmly packed brown sugar
1 teaspoon all-purpose flour
½ teaspoon salt
1 cup chopped walnuts
¾ cup semisweet chocolate morsels
½ cup chopped dates
Cinnamon Whipped Cream (recipe follows)

Roll half of pastry to ⅛" thickness on a lightly floured surface. Place in 9" pie plate. Roll remaining pastry to ⅛" thickness; cut into small leaves and stems, using a cookie cutter or a small knife. Moisten the edge of piecrust with water and gently press cutouts around the edge. Set aside any remaining cutouts.

Combine corn syrup, eggs, and vanilla in large mixing bowl. Combine brown sugar, flour, and salt; add to corn syrup mixture, stirring until well blended. Stir in walnuts.

Sprinkle chocolate morsels and dates evenly in pastry shell. Pour walnut mixture over chocolate and dates. Arrange reserved cutouts over filling. Bake at 350° for 35 minutes or until filling is set. Cool completely. To serve, slice and top with Cinnamon Whipped Cream. Yield: 1 (9") pie.

Cinnamon Whipped Cream:

½ cup whipping cream
2 tablespoons powdered sugar
½ teaspoon ground cinnamon
½ cup sour cream

Combine first 3 ingredients in a medium bowl; beat until stiff peaks form. Fold in sour cream and chill thoroughly. Yield: 1⅓ cups.

Right: Extraordinary pastry crusts make these pies more than delicious. The tightly woven lattice crust tops scrumptious Rum Raisin Apple Tarts. A foliage pastry garland encircles the Chocolate-Date Walnut Pie. Twisting pastry winds around the Praline-Topped Pear Pie. (See the box on page 85 for instructions on how to make the dried apple garland.)

Praline-Topped Pear Pie

Pastry for double-crust 9" pie
1 (8-ounce) carton sour cream
1 egg, lightly beaten
1 teaspoon vanilla extract
½ teaspoon freshly grated nutmeg
¾ cup sugar
3 tablespoons all-purpose flour
¼ teaspoon salt
5 cups peeled, sliced pears
Praline Topping (recipe follows)

Roll half of pastry to ⅛" thickness on a lightly floured surface. Place the rolled pastry in a 9" pie plate; set aside.

Combine sour cream, egg, vanilla, and nutmeg in a large mixing bowl; mix well. Combine sugar, flour, and salt; add to sour cream mixture. Beat mixture with a wire whisk until smooth. Stir pears into mixture. Spoon mixture into pastry shell.

Roll remaining pastry to ⅛" thickness; transfer to top of pie. Trim off excess pastry along edges and fold under.

Cut ¼"-wide strips from excess pastry. Moisten edge of piecrust with water. Interlace strips along moistened edge; gently press to adhere strips to edge.

Cut slits in top of crust for steam to escape. Bake at 400° for 30 minutes; remove from oven and crumble Praline Topping over top crust. Bake an additional 10 minutes or until topping melts. Cool completely. Yield: 1 (9") pie.

Praline Topping:

⅓ cup firmly packed brown sugar
¼ cup all-purpose flour
½ teaspoon ground cinnamon
¼ cup butter or margarine, cut into small pieces
¼ cup chopped pecans, toasted

Combine brown sugar, flour, and cinnamon in a small bowl. Cut in butter with a pastry blender until mixture resembles coarse meal. Stir pecans into mixture. Yield: 1 cup.

Sweet Potato and Macadamia Nut Tart

Pastry for single-crust 9" pie
3 medium sweet potatoes
¾ cup firmly packed brown sugar, divided
3 tablespoons butter or margarine
¼ cup brandy
1 tablespoon lemon juice
1 teaspoon vanilla extract
⅔ cup macadamia nuts, chopped
2 tablespoons all-purpose flour
2 tablespoons butter or margarine, melted

Roll pastry to ⅛" thickness on a lightly floured surface. Place in an ungreased 9½" tart pan with removable sides. Bake at 350° for 5 minutes. Set aside.

Cook potatoes in boiling water 15 minutes. Let cool to touch; peel and slice into ¼"-thick slices. Arrange in pastry shell and sprinkle with ½ cup brown sugar. Dot with butter.

Combine brandy, lemon juice, and vanilla in a small saucepan; bring to a boil. Pour evenly over potato slices. Bake at 325° for 45 minutes.

Combine macadamia nuts, remaining ¼ cup brown sugar, flour, and butter, stirring well; sprinkle evenly over tart. Bake an additional 10 minutes or until pastry is golden brown. Cool completely. Yield: 1 (9½") tart.

Lemon Slice Custard Pie

2 medium lemons
1¾ cups plus 2 teaspoons sugar, divided
Pastry for double-crust 9" pie
2 tablespoons plus 2 teaspoons all-purpose flour
¼ teaspoon salt
¼ cup butter or margarine, melted
4 eggs, lightly beaten
1 tablespoon lemon juice
1 egg white, beaten
1 teaspoon sugar

Freeze lemons for 2 hours. Cut lemons into quarters lengthwise. Using a sharp knife, cut lemon quarters into ⅛"-thick slices. Remove and discard seeds.

Combine lemon slices and 1¾ cups sugar; stir well. Let stand 2 hours.

Roll half of pastry to ⅛" thickness on a lightly

floured surface. Place in a 9" pie plate. Set aside.

Combine flour and salt in a large bowl; add butter, eggs, and lemon juice, stirring well. Stir in 1 teaspoon sugar and lemon slice mixture. Pour into pastry shell.

Roll remaining pastry to ⅛" thickness; transfer to top of pie. Trim off excess pastry along edges. Fold edges under and flute. Cut slits in top of crust for steam to escape. Brush pastry with egg white; sprinkle with remaining 1 teaspoon sugar. Bake at 400° for 15 minutes. Reduce heat to 350° and bake an additional 20 minutes or until golden brown. Cool completely. Yield: 1 (9") pie.

Cranberry and Spice Pie

1 (12-ounce) bag fresh cranberries
1 cup water
2 cups sugar
¼ cup cornstarch
¾ teaspoon ground cinnamon
½ teaspoon ground nutmeg
⅛ teaspoon salt
¼ cup butter or margarine
1 teaspoon vanilla extract
Pastry for double-crust 9" pie
Wreath stencil (pattern on page 151)
Egg Yolk Paint (recipe follows)

Combine cranberries and water in a large saucepan; bring to a boil. Reduce heat, cover, and simmer 5 minutes. Combine sugar, cornstarch, cinnamon, nutmeg, and salt, stirring well. Add to cranberry mixture, stirring until well blended. Cook over medium heat, stirring constantly, until mixture is thickened and bubbly. Remove from heat; add butter and vanilla, stirring gently until butter melts. Cool slightly.

Roll half of pastry to ⅛" thickness on a lightly floured surface. Place in a 9" pie plate. Spoon cranberry mixture into pastry shell; set aside.

Roll remaining pastry to ⅛" thickness. To make stencil, transfer wreath pattern to heavy paper. Cut out and place on top of crust. Using a small paintbrush, paint inside cutout openings onto top crust with Egg Yolk Paint. Let dry 5 minutes. Carefully place stenciled top crust over filling. Trim off excess pastry along edges. Fold edges under and flute. Cut slits in top of crust for steam to escape. Bake at 400° for 20 minutes; reduce heat to 350° and bake an additional 30 minutes or until lightly browned. Cool completely. Yield: 1 (9") pie.

Egg Yolk Paint:

1 egg yolk, beaten
¼ teaspoon water
Red, green liquid or paste food coloring

Combine egg yolk and water; stir well. Divide mixture in half; tint with coloring. Keep paint covered until ready to use. If paint thickens, stir in a few drops of water. Yield: enough paint for 1 (9") stencil.

Apple Garland Accent

This cheerful apple, cranberry, and bay leaf garland bears the colors of Christmas with home-style appeal.

There are several ways to dehydrate apples. We tried two—using a microwave oven and using a dehydrator. The easiest way to dry apples is in a dehydrator, an appliance that is available at kitchen and variety stores. It is designed so that air circulates freely between vented racks, drying the fruit in a few hours. The microwave oven method works just as well, but requires more attention.

To prepare the fruit for either method, core the apples (do not peel); then, using a very sharp knife, slice into ⅛-inch slices. Sprinkle both sides of the slices lightly with ascorbic-citric powder to prevent discoloration. Dehydrate fruit slices using one of the following methods:

Microwave oven: Place slices on a paper towel on a microwave-safe plate. Microwave on HIGH for two minutes. Then, with a paper towel in each hand, pat slices to remove excess moisture. Turn slices over and continue process until moisture is almost entirely absorbed. Slide slices onto a wooden dowel and let dry naturally until moisture is completely gone. Slices should feel leathery.

Dehydrator: Following manufacturer's directions, place slices one inch apart on the racks of the dehydrator and allow to aerate for three to four hours, until fruit is leathery. Slices should be completely dry.

To make the garland, use a sturdy needle and thread and string dehydrated apple slices, bay leaves, and fresh cranberries in the desired pattern and length. Tie a bow to each end of the garland.

Apricot Cheese Tart

8 (4") tart shells, unbaked
1 (6-ounce) package dried apricots
2 cups water
⅔ cup sugar, divided
1 tablespoon frozen orange juice concentrate, thawed
½ teaspoon ground cinnamon
Dash of freshly ground nutmeg
5 ounces cream cheese, softened
1 egg
3 tablespoons sour cream
1½ teaspoons vanilla extract
Apricot roses (optional)
Orange rind curls (optional)

Bake tart shells at 350° for 5 minutes; set aside.

Combine apricots and water in a medium saucepan; bring to boil. Reduce heat and simmer 30 minutes. Drain.

Position knife blade in food processor bowl; add apricots and process until coarsely chopped. Combine apricots, ⅓ cup sugar, orange juice concentrate, cinnamon, and nutmeg; stir well and set aside.

Beat cream cheese at high speed of an electric mixer until light and fluffy. Gradually add remaining ⅓ cup sugar, 1 tablespoon at a time, beating until well blended. Add egg and sour cream, beating at low speed until well combined. Stir in vanilla.

Spoon apricot mixture evenly into partially baked tart shells; top with cream cheese mixture. Bake at 350° for 20 minutes or until pastry is golden. Cool completely on wire rack. Garnish with apricot roses and orange rind curls, if desired. Yield: 8 (4") tarts.

Strawberry-Rhubarb Tart

Pastry for double-crust 9" pie
1 cup plus 1 tablespoon sugar
3 tablespoons cornstarch
⅛ teaspoon freshly grated nutmeg
⅓ cup frozen apple juice concentrate, thawed
2 tablespoons butter or margarine
4 cups sliced fresh rhubarb
2 cups halved fresh strawberries
¼ teaspoon ground cinnamon
1 egg white, lightly beaten

Roll two-thirds of pastry to ⅛" thickness. Fit pastry into an 11" x 7½" x 1" tart pan; chill 30 minutes. Keep remaining pastry covered and chilled.

Combine 1 cup sugar, cornstarch, and nutmeg in a large saucepan. Stir in apple juice concentrate. Cook over medium heat, stirring constantly, until thickened and bubbly. Remove from heat, add butter, and stir until butter melts. Fold in rhubarb and strawberries. Spoon into prepared pastry shell.

Roll remaining third of pastry to ⅛" thickness on a lightly floured surface. Cut a 12" x 2" and an 8" x 2" strip of pastry; place pastry strips on filling perpendicular to each other, so that they look like ribbons on a gift package. (Refer to photograph on page 80.) Seal ends to sides of tart. Make a bow from remaining pastry; place bow where 2 strips cross.

Combine remaining 1 tablespoon sugar and cinnamon; stir well. Brush pastry with egg white and sprinkle with sugar mixture. Bake at 425° for 10 minutes; reduce heat to 350° and bake an additional 30 minutes or until golden brown. Cool completely. Yield: 1 (11" x 7½") tart.

Basic Pastry

1 cup all-purpose flour
¼ teaspoon salt
¼ cup plus 2 tablespoons shortening
2 to 3 tablespoons cold water

Combine flour and salt in a small mixing bowl; cut in shortening with a pastry blender until mixture resembles coarse meal.

Sprinkle cold water, 1 tablespoon at a time, evenly over surface; stir with a fork until dry ingredients are moistened. Shape into a ball; chill. Yield: pastry for 1 (9") single-crust pie.

Double-Crust Cheddar Pastry

2 cups all-purpose flour
½ teaspoon salt
½ cup plus 1 tablespoon butter or margarine
¾ cup (3 ounces) shredded sharp Cheddar cheese
3 to 4 tablespoons cold water

Combine flour and salt in a small mixing bowl. Cut butter and cheese into the flour mixture with a pastry blender until the mixture resembles coarse meal. Sprinkle cold water, 1 tablespoon at a time, evenly over surface. Stir the mixture with a fork until the dry ingredients are moistened. Shape the mixture into a ball and chill. Yield: pastry for 1 (9") double-crust pie.

Below: Nuts from sunny Hawaii add an unexpected crunch to this Sweet Potato and Macadamia Nut Tart.

Toasted Nut Pastry

½ cup chopped pecans, walnuts, or hazelnuts, toasted
1 cup all-purpose flour
¼ teaspoon ground cinnamon
¼ teaspoon salt
⅓ cup plus 2 tablespoons shortening
3 to 4 tablespoons cold water

Position knife blade in food processor bowl; add nuts and process until coarsely ground.

Combine ground nuts, flour, cinnamon, and salt in a medium mixing bowl; cut in shortening with a pastry blender until mixture resembles coarse meal. Sprinkle cold water, 1 tablespoon at time, evenly over surface; stir with a fork until dry ingredients are moistened. Shape into a ball; chill. Yield: pastry for 1 (9") single-crust pie.

Oatmeal Pastry

½ cup regular oats, uncooked
1 cup all-purpose flour
2 tablespoons brown sugar
½ teaspoon salt
¼ cup shortening
¼ cup butter
3 to 4 tablespoons cold water

Position knife blade in food processor bowl; add oats and pulse 2 to 3 times or until oats are coarsely ground. Remove and set aside 2 tablespoons ground oats. Continue processing until oats are finely ground.

Combine coarsely ground and finely ground oats, flour, sugar, and salt in a small mixing bowl; cut in shortening and butter with pastry blender until mixture resembles coarse meal. Sprinkle cold water, 1 tablespoon at a time, evenly over surface; stir with a fork until dry ingredients are moistened. Shape into a ball; chill. Yield: pastry for 1 (9") single-crust pie.

Whole Wheat Pastry

¾ cup whole wheat flour
¼ cup plus 2 tablespoons all-purpose flour
½ teaspoon salt
½ cup shortening
3 to 4 tablespoons cold water

Combine first 3 ingredients in a medium mixing bowl; cut in shortening with a pastry blender until mixture resembles coarse meal. Sprinkle cold water, 1 tablespoon at a time, evenly over surface; stir with a fork until dry ingredients are moistened. Shape into a ball; chill. Yield: pastry for 1 (9") single-crust pie.

Left: A simple-to-stencil holly wreath turns basic pastry into holiday magic. The recipe for this Cranberry and Spice Pie and the stenciling instructions are on 85.

Woodburned Ivy Platter

The woodburned ivy meandering around the edges of this purchased wooden platter creates a holiday look with simplicity.

A 13½-inch-diameter wooden platter and a woodburning pen are the main materials needed to complete this project. Using graphite paper, transfer the pattern on page 151 to the platter; repeat the pattern around the edge to complete the border.

Woodburn along the outlines. Use the tip of the woodburning pen to make the finer leaf veins. Use the broad side of the tip of the woodburning pen to make the thicker leaf outlines and stems.

After you have completed this beginner project, expand your woodburning skills with a variety of designs. Embellish a cheese board with geometric patterns or shapes from nature. Or you might decorate a wooden canister set with an enlarged version of the decorative jar patterns on page 150.

Holiday Showstoppers

An old-world Christmas custom paired roast peacock and boar as main entrées. A wise hostess today will offer a smashing alternative to traditional turkey for special get-togethers during the holidays. Here are several fine centerpieces, including Marinated Beef Tenderloin with Mustard Cream, Fruited Crown Roast of Pork, and Pepper-Crusted Standing Rib with Yorkshire Pudding.

Below: Every guest will dine like royalty when served Fruited Crown Roast of Pork.

90

Fruited Crown Roast of Pork

1 (6-ounce) package long-grain and wild
   rice mix
1½ cups apple juice, divided
½ cup firmly packed brown sugar, divided
1 cup pitted prunes, halved
1 cup dried apricots, quartered
¾ cup Madeira
Dash of ground cloves
½ cup Dijon mustard
1 (16-rib) crown roast of pork
Salt and pepper
Parsley sprigs
Apricot roses
1 tablespoon cornstarch

Cook rice according to package directions; set
aside.

Combine ¾ cup apple juice, ¼ cup brown sugar,
prunes, apricots, Madeira, and cloves in a medium
saucepan; bring to a boil. Cover, reduce heat, and
simmer 15 minutes. Uncover and simmer an additional 15 minutes. Combine rice and fruit mixture;
stir well.

Combine mustard and remaining ¼ cup brown
sugar; spread mixture evenly over surface of roast.
Sprinkle with salt and pepper. Place roast, bone ends
up, on a rack in a shallow roasting pan. Insert meat
thermometer, making sure it does not touch fat or
bone.

Spoon rice mixture into center of roast. Cover
stuffing and exposed ends of ribs with aluminum foil.
Bake at 325° for 2½ hours or until thermometer
registers 160°, basting with ½ cup apple juice every
15 minutes.

Remove roast to serving platter; let stand 15
minutes. Garnish roast with parsley sprigs and apricot
roses. Skim fat from pan drippings. Combine remaining ¼ cup apple juice and cornstarch; stir well and
add to pan drippings.

Cook over medium heat, stirring constantly, until
smooth and thick. Serve sauce with roast and stuffing. Yield: 8 servings.

Marinated Beef Tenderloin with Mustard Cream

1 small onion, thinly sliced
1 cup soy sauce
1 cup dry sherry
½ cup vegetable oil
¼ cup firmly packed brown sugar
2 tablespoons lemon juice
1 teaspoon peeled grated gingerroot
1 teaspoon freshly ground pepper
1 (5- to 6-pound) beef tenderloin, trimmed
Watercress (optional)
Cherry tomatoes (optional)
Mustard Cream (recipe follows)

Combine first 8 ingredients; stir well. Place tenderloin in large shallow dish; pour marinade over
tenderloin. Cover and marinate in refrigerator 8
hours, turning occasionally.

Uncover tenderloin; drain off and reserve marinade. Place tenderloin on a rack in a roasting pan;
insert meat thermometer into thickest portion of
tenderloin, making sure it does not touch fat. Bake at
425° for 50 minutes or until thermometer registers
140° (rare), 150° (medium-rare), or 160° (medium),
basting occasionally with marinade. Remove to a
serving platter. Garnish with watercress and cherry
tomatoes, if desired. Serve with Mustard Cream.
Yield: 10 to 12 servings.

Mustard Cream:

½ cup whipping cream
1 tablespoon plus 2 teaspoons dry mustard
1 (8-ounce) carton sour cream
2 tablespoons white wine vinegar
2 teaspoons sugar
¼ teaspoon salt

Combine whipping cream and dry mustard in a
small bowl; let stand 10 minutes. Stir in sour cream
and remaining ingredients. Cover and chill thoroughly. Yield: 1½ cups.

Sage and Garlic Leg of Lamb with Almond-Orzo Pilaf

1 pod fresh garlic, separated into cloves
2 tablespoons rubbed sage
3 tablespoons olive oil
1 teaspoon salt
1 teaspoon pepper
1 (6- to 7-pound) leg of lamb
1 lemon, cut in half
Fresh sage (optional)
Spiced crabapples (optional)
Almond-Orzo Pilaf (recipe follows)

Combine garlic, sage, olive oil, salt, and pepper in container of an electric blender. Top blender with cover and process until smooth. Set aside.

Place lamb, fat side up, on a rack in a shallow roasting pan. Rub surface of lamb with lemon. Make slits, about ½" deep, on outside of lamb. Stuff garlic mixture evenly into slits; spread any remaining garlic mixture over surface of lamb. Insert meat thermometer, making sure it does not touch fat or bone. Bake at 325° for 2½ to 3 hours or until meat thermometer registers 160°.

Transfer lamb to a serving platter and let stand 10 minutes before carving. Garnish with fresh sage and crabapples, if desired. Serve with Almond-Orzo Pilaf. Yield: 8 to 10 servings.

Almond-Orzo Pilaf:

1 green onion, minced
4 cloves garlic, minced
3 tablespoons chopped fresh parsley
1 tablespoon olive oil
2 tablespoons brandy
4 cups hot cooked orzo
¼ cup slivered almonds, toasted
Salt and pepper to taste

Sauté onion, garlic, and parsley in olive oil until tender. Stir in brandy. Combine orzo, almonds, and salt and pepper in a large bowl. Add garlic mixture, tossing gently. Yield: 4½ cups.

Pepper-Crusted Standing Rib with Yorkshire Pudding

¼ cup whole black peppercorns
3 tablespoons juniper berries
1 tablespoon vegetable oil, divided
1 (8-pound) standing rib roast
1¼ pounds pearl onions
6 medium-size sweet red peppers, seeded and halved
4 medium Anaheim chile peppers, seeded and halved
Curly endive
Yorkshire Pudding (recipe follows)

Position knife blade in food processor bowl; add peppercorns and juniper berries. Process until coarsely ground; set aside. Brush 2 teaspoons oil over surface of roast. Sprinkle half of peppercorn mixture evenly over roast. Place roast, fat side up, on a rack in a shallow roasting pan. Insert meat thermometer, making sure it does not touch fat or bone. Bake at 325° for 2 hours.

Combine remaining 1 teaspoon oil and remaining peppercorn mixture in a large bowl; stir well. Add onions and peppers, tossing gently.

Spoon vegetable mixture evenly around roast. Continue baking 1 hour or until meat thermometer registers 140° (rare), 160° (medium), or 170° (well done).

Remove roast and vegetables to a serving platter, reserving ¼ cup clear pan drippings to make Yorkshire Pudding. Garnish roast with endive, and serve with Yorkshire Pudding. Yield: 10 to 12 servings.

Cooking Tips

Beef, pork, and lamb should be roasted in heavy roasting pans to allow for proper heat distribution and ease of handling.

Roasts weighing more than three pounds should be removed from the oven when they are within five degrees of desired temperature. (Use a meat thermometer to determine.) When a roast is removed from the oven and allowed to rest at room temperature for 10 minutes, the temperature will rise approximately five degrees before leveling and cooling off. This resting period allows the meat to reabsorb its juices and settle before carving—the result: a delectably tender and juicy entrée!

Yorkshire Pudding:

1 cup all-purpose flour
¼ teaspoon salt
1 cup milk
2 eggs, slightly beaten
Vegetable cooking spray
¼ cup beef pan drippings

Combine first 4 ingredients; beat at low speed of an electric mixer just until smooth.

Coat muffin pans with cooking spray. Spoon 1 teaspoon pan drippings into each muffin pan; tilt to coat evenly. Spoon batter into muffin pans, filling half full. Bake at 425° for 15 minutes. Reduce heat to 350°, and bake an additional 18 to 20 minutes. Serve immediately. Yield: 1 dozen.

Selecting Choice Cuts

Since you may pay a premium price for your holiday meat, be sure to get the fine quality that you are expecting. At least a week ahead of time, seek the advice of the head butcher at your grocery. Tell him the type of cut suggested in the recipe. This will allow time to special-order the meat, if necessary.

There are certain qualities to look for when making your holiday meat selection. Beef should have a healthy deep red color and firm white fat. Tender roast should have adequate marbling. This network of fat plays an important role in self-basting the meat during roasting.

Beef should always appear to be moist and firm in texture.

Pork should have a bright pink color. The bones should be pale pink and the fat firm and white.

Lamb should have a bright pink color, pink bones, and white fat. The fell, which is the tissue-like covering over the surface of lamb roasts, should be left in place. It acts as a cover to hold in the juices as the lamb cooks.

As a general rule, a pound of boneless meat will serve four people, while a pound of meat with a moderate amount of bone will serve two to three people. Have the butcher trim excess or surface fat to ⅛-inch thickness.

Below: This Pepper-Crusted Standing Rib is accompanied by the traditional Yorkshire Pudding, a side dish invented in northern England to use up precious meat drippings. Not really a pudding at all, Yorkshire Pudding is similar to popovers.

Pepper-Glazed Pork Roast

1 (6- to 7-pound) pork loin roast
2 teaspoons salt
1 teaspoon onion powder
1 teaspoon garlic powder
½ teaspoon pepper
8 medium-size sweet potatoes, peeled
   and quartered
1 cup water
2 medium onions, sliced and separated
   into rings
½ cup orange marmalade
½ cup hot jalapeño jelly
4 oranges, peeled and sliced
¼ cup water
3 tablespoons all-purpose flour

Trim excess fat from roast. Combine salt, onion powder, garlic powder, and pepper; rub mixture over surface of roast. Place the roast on a rack in a shallow roasting pan; insert the meat thermometer, making sure it does not touch bone or fat. Bake at 350° for 1 hour.

Cook potatoes in boiling water to cover 20 minutes or until just tender. Pour 1 cup water in roasting pan; place potatoes and onion rings around roast. Combine marmalade and jelly; brush over roast and vegetables. Bake 1 additional hour or until meat thermometer registers 160°.

Remove roast to serving platter; let stand 10 minutes. Remove vegetables with a slotted spoon and arrange around roast. Skim fat from pan drippings; add oranges and stir until oranges are warm. Remove oranges with slotted spoon and transfer to serving platter.

Combine ¼ cup water and flour; stir well. Add to pan drippings. Cook over medium heat, stirring constantly, until smooth and thick. Serve with roast. Yield: 16 servings.

Perfect Presentation

If you choose to serve one of these entrées at your holiday dinner table, plan ahead. Have available a very sharp, straight-edged knife and learn the proper carving techniques before you are in the limelight as the carver. Follow the simple directions below for fail-safe carving.

Standing Rib Beef Roast: Place roast on its flat side on the serving platter. Insert your carving fork just below the first rib. Slice horizontally from the fat side of the meat to the rib bone. Slice vertically along the rib bone to release each slice. Slide knife under each slice; lift and remove slice to plate.

Beef Tenderloin: Place roast on serving platter. Slice meat crosswise into one-inch-thick slices.

Pork Loin Roast: Place roast on serving platter with rib side down. Slice meat vertically from fat side to rib bone. Slice along rib bone to release each slice and transfer to plate using carving knife and fork.

Crown Roast of Pork: Place roast on serving platter, with ends of rib bones facing up. Slice roast vertically between ribs. Each serving should have one rib.

Carefully transfer slices to plate, using the carving knife and fork.

Leg of Lamb: Place shank bone to your right. Cut two to three slices from thin side, parallel to leg bone. Turn leg over so that it rests on this cut side. Steady the leg with a carving fork and make vertical slices down to leg bone. Cut along the leg bone to release each slice; lift and remove slice to plate.

Noah's Ginger Ark

½ cup shortening
¼ cup sugar
¼ cup firmly packed brown sugar
1 egg
½ cup molasses
3 cups all-purpose flour
½ teaspoon baking soda
½ teaspoon salt
½ teaspoon ground cinnamon
½ teaspoon ground ginger
½ teaspoon ground nutmeg
½ teaspoon ground cloves
½ teaspoon grated orange rind
pattern and placement diagram on page 152
1 (11" x 17") piece of paper
2" gingerbread woman cookie cutter
2" heart cookie cutter
1¼" star cookie cutter
11 commercial animal crackers
Silver dragées
2 large paper clips (optional)
45" (¼"-wide) red ribbon (optional)

Cream shortening; gradually add sugars, beating at medium speed of an electric mixer until light and fluffy. Add egg, beating well. Add molasses, beating well. Combine flour and next 7 ingredients; stir well and add to creamed mixture, beating at low speed of an electric mixer. Cover and chill dough 1 hour.

Reserve a third of dough. On a lightly floured baking sheet, roll remaining two-thirds of dough to a 13" x 10" rectangle, ¼" thick.

Transfer pattern to paper and cut out. Transfer outline of pattern to dough. Cut ark from dough using a sharp knife, reserving dough scraps. To add details to dough, refer to pattern and Placement Diagram for the following: Using a knife, score bottom of roof line and top of hull. (Do *not* cut all the way through dough.) Score the door and windows. On hull, score lines to resemble wooden planks. Rotate baking sheet so that cookie is upside down. Referring to photograph and using edge of a rounded measuring spoon, make scallop marks on roof, starting at roof line and working towards top edge.

Roll half of dough scraps into a 16" rope. Place along top edge of hull. Roll remaining half of scraps into a 16½" rope. Cut an 11½" piece from rope and transfer to bottom of roof line. Shape remaining 5"

piece into an arch and place over door. Press ropes gently in place. Using a toothpick, make small diagonal marks along ropes.

Roll remaining third of dough to ⅛" thickness on a lightly floured surface. Using cookie cutter, cut out 1 gingerbread woman (to resemble a robed Noah). Brush underside of Noah cookie with water and place in door of ark. Using a toothpick, make small dots in dough for features, hair, and beard on Noah. Using a knife, score 2 lines across bottom of robe. Cut out heart and stars with cookie cutters; brush undersides with water and place on ark according to pattern. Use toothpick to make indentations in heart as shown. Brush undersides of animal crackers with water and place on ark. Decorate ark with silver dragées.

Note: If you wish to hang the cookie for display, before baking, insert 2 paper clips deep into top edge of ark, where indicated on pattern. Reinforce cookie by pressing a small piece of dough to back of ark over area where each paper clip is inserted.

Bake at 300° for 30 minutes or until golden brown. Gently loosen from cookie sheet; let cool on cookie sheet 10 minutes. Remove to wire rack and cool completely.

Cut a 20" piece of ribbon. Knot 1 end of ribbon securely around each paper clip. Cut remaining ribbon in half and tie a bow around each paper clip.

A Harvest of Gifts

Whether your harvest comes from the garden or the grocery store, these nut and fruit butters, conserves, and compotes become gifts from the heart.

Make-Your-Own Nut Butter

**2 cups roasted, unsalted cashews, peanuts,
   or almonds
1 tablespoon peanut oil
½ teaspoon salt (optional)**

Position knife blade in food processor bowl; add cashews, oil, and salt, if desired. Top with cover and process 1 minute and 30 seconds or until mixture forms a ball, scraping sides of processor bowl once.

Store in refrigerator. Yield: about 1¼ cups.

Note: For chunky nut butters, stir in ½ cup chopped cashews, peanuts, or almonds after processing the mixture.

Oven-Baked Pine-Apple Butter

**3 cups apple cider
2 cups sugar
1 (8-ounce) can crushed pineapple, undrained
1 teaspoon ground cinnamon
5 pounds cooking apples, peeled, cored,
   and sliced**

Combine first 4 ingredients in a large oven-proof Dutch oven; bring to a boil. Stir in apples. Cover and bake at 350° for 3 hours, stirring once. Uncover and cool 15 minutes.

Position knife blade in food processor bowl; add a fourth of apple mixture. Top with cover and process

until smooth. Repeat with remaining apple mixture in quarters.

Return puréed mixture to Dutch oven. Bake an additional 2 hours or until mixture thickens and is golden brown, stirring twice.

Spoon hot mixture into hot sterilized jars, leaving ¼" headspace. Remove air bubbles and wipe jar rims. Cover at once with metal lids and screw on bands. Process in boiling-water bath 10 minutes. Yield: 7 half-pints.

Sweet Cream Pumpkin Butter

2 cups whipping cream
1 (3") piece vanilla bean
2 (1-pound) pumpkins
1½ cups firmly packed brown sugar

Bring whipping cream to a boil in a heavy saucepan. Reduce heat and simmer, uncovered, 20 minutes or until whipping cream reduces to 1 cup. Cool completely.

Split vanilla bean piece in half lengthwise; scrape vanilla seeds from bean. Stir seeds into whipping cream; set aside.

Cut pumpkins in half crosswise; remove and discard seeds. Peel and cut pumpkins into 1" cubes. Place pumpkin in a large Dutch oven; add water to cover. Bring to a boil; cover, reduce heat, and simmer 30 minutes or until pumpkin is tender. Drain well.

Position knife blade in food processor bowl. Add half of pumpkin; top with cover and process until smooth. Repeat procedure with remaining pumpkin. Return pumpkin to Dutch oven; stir in sugar. Cook over medium heat 10 minutes or until mixture thickens and mounds from a spoon, stirring occasionally. Remove from heat, and cool slightly; stir in whipped cream mixture. Chill.

Spoon mixture into sterilized jars. Remove air bubbles and wipe jar rims.Cover with metal lids and screw on bands. Store up to 2 weeks in refrigerator. Yield: 4 half-pints.

Left: For a gift with everlasting appeal, serve up these relishes, compotes, and fruit and nut butters in hand-painted containers. Instructions for decorative jars are on page 99.

97

Dried-Fruit Butter

2 (8-ounce) packages dried apricots
2 (8-ounce) packages dried apple slices
2 cups dried cranberries
1½ cups orange juice
¼ cup honey
2 tablespoons lemon juice
4 cups sugar

Place apricots, apple slices, and cranberries in a large bowl. Cover with water 2" above fruit; let stand at room temperature 8 hours. Drain.

Combine fruit, orange juice, honey, and lemon juice in a Dutch oven. Bring to a boil; reduce heat and simmer, uncovered, 30 minutes or until fruit is tender.

Position knife blade in food processor bowl; add a third of fruit mixture. Top with cover and process until smooth. Repeat process with remaining fruit mixture in thirds. Return fruit mixture to Dutch oven; add sugar, stirring well. Cook, uncovered, over medium-low heat until mixture thickens and mounds from a spoon, stirring occasionally.

Spoon mixture into hot sterilized jars, leaving ¼" headspace. Remove air bubbles and wipe jar rims. Cover at once with metal lids and screw on bands. Process in boiling-water bath 10 minutes. Yield: 10 half-pints.

Horseradish Salsa

1 cup vinegar
¼ cup water
¼ cup firmly packed brown sugar
2 tablespoons prepared horseradish
14 medium tomatoes, peeled, seeded, and chopped
1 cup chopped celery
½ cup chopped green pepper
½ cup chopped onion
1 jalapeño pepper, seeded and finely chopped

Combine first 4 ingredients in a large Dutch oven; bring to a boil. Reduce heat; cover and simmer 10 minutes.

Add tomatoes and remaining ingredients; bring to a boil. Reduce heat; cover and simmer 10 minutes.

Spoon mixture into hot sterilized jars, leaving ½" headspace. Remove air bubbles and wipe jar rims.

Cover at once with metal lids and screw on bands. Process in boiling-water bath 15 minutes. Yield: 10 half-pints.

Rhubarb and Pecan Conserve

2 pounds fresh rhubarb, sliced
2 cups sugar
1 cup raisins
1 cup white grape juice
2 tablespoons grated orange rind
⅔ cup fresh orange juice
2 cups chopped pecans

Combine fresh rhubarb, sugar, raisins, white grape juice, orange rind, and orange juice in a large Dutch oven; stir well. Bring to a boil; cover, reduce heat, and simmer 30 minutes or until mixture thickens, stirring frequently. Stir in pecans.

Spoon mixture into hot sterilized jars, leaving ¼" headspace. Remove air bubbles and wipe jar rims. Cover at once with metal lids and screw on bands. Process in boiling-water bath 15 minutes. Yield: 6 half-pints.

Brandied Cranberry Compote

1 lemon, thinly sliced
10 whole cloves
1 (3") stick cinnamon
3 cups water
1 (12-ounce) package fresh cranberries
1 cup pitted prunes, coarsely chopped
1 cup dried apple slices, coarsely chopped
¾ cup sugar
½ cup golden raisins
½ cup currants
½ cup brandy

Combine lemon, cloves, and cinnamon in a cheesecloth bag. Combine cheesecloth bag, water, and next 6 ingredients in a Dutch oven; stir well. Bring to a boil. Reduce heat and simmer, uncovered, until apple is tender. Remove and discard cheesecloth bag. Stir in brandy. Spoon mixture into hot, sterilized jars, leaving ½" headspace. Remove air bubbles and wipe jar rims. Cover at once with metal lids and screw on bands. Process in boiling-water bath 10 minutes. Yield: 5 half-pints.

Tri-Color Pepper Relish

1½ cups vinegar
1 cup water
¾ cup sugar
1 (2") piece fresh ginger, peeled
1 teaspoon salt
4 cups chopped green pepper
4 cups chopped sweet red pepper
4 cups chopped sweet yellow pepper
1½ cups chopped onion

Combine first 5 ingredients in a Dutch oven; bring to a boil. Reduce heat, cover, and simmer 15 minutes.

Remove and discard ginger. Add remaining ingredients; stir well. Bring to a boil; reduce heat, cover, and simmer 15 minutes.

Spoon mixture into hot sterilized jars, leaving ¼" headspace. Remove air bubbles and wipe jar rims. Cover at once with metal lids and screw on bands. Process in boiling-water bath 5 minutes. Yield: 12 half-pints.

Decorative Painted Jars

By painting glass jars and their lids with enamel paints, and then sealing the paints with low heat, you can recycle empties as charming gifts.

You can decorate your jars using one of three ways mentioned here. Before painting, clean the jars and lids thoroughly with detergent and warm water to remove all dust, dirt, and glue. Allow jars and lids to dry.

To decorate the lids, lay newspapers on a large surface and, following manufacturer's instructions, spray-paint with white enamel. Allow paint to dry completely.

Using a tailors' pen, trace the patterns on page 150 onto the lids. Paint your design with enamel paints, let dry, and then highlight with a gold metallic marker.

Remove unwanted pen marks with a damp cloth. Following manufacturer's instructions, seal the paint on the lids with spray varnish.

You can also paint designs onto the jar itself. Free-hand simple scenes or slip a pattern into the jar and paint the design that shows through.

Finally, the easiest way to embellish jars is by simply painting over textures, following patterns already pressed into the glass. The waffle weave on home-canning jelly jars and textures pressed into fancy honey jars are good examples of glass designs. Use your paintbrush to follow the outline on the glass and highlight the design with a gold marker.

To keep the paint from wearing off, place the jars in a 200-degree oven for 30 minutes.

Allow the jars to cool slowly to room temperature by leaving them in the oven, turning off the heat, and opening the oven door slightly.

Gently hand-wash the jars; an automatic dishwasher will cause the paint to peel.

Above: A centerpiece of dried flowers, pomegranates, and gilded artichokes tucked into soft green moss gives a woodsy atmosphere to this table of treats. From top right, Chesapeake Hot Crab Dip, Swiss Vegetable Puffs, Pepper-Marinated Olives, Tiger Fudge, Chive Dip with Pasta and Vegetable Kabobs, and Cranberry Gin Spritzers.

A Party with a Plan

Chesapeake Hot Crab Dip • Swiss Vegetable Puffs
Chive Dip with Pasta and Vegetable Kabobs
Garlic Cheese Pâté • Pepper-Marinated Olives
Tiger Fudge • Spiced Rum Slush
Cranberry Gin Spritzers

The nonstop bustle of the holidays makes planning crucial to successful entertaining. Here are eight mouth-watering recipes that can be made well in advance. With most of the cooking behind you, you can spend more time with your loved ones and less time in the kitchen.

Chesapeake Hot Crab Dip

4 shallots, minced
¼ cup plus 2 tablespoons butter or margarine,
    melted
3 tablespoons all-purpose flour
1½ cups milk
1 cup whipping cream
½ cup Cognac
1 tablespoon plus 1 teaspoon white
    wine Worcestershire sauce
2 teaspoons lemon juice
½ teaspoon salt
¼ teaspoon ground white pepper
2 pounds fresh lump crabmeat, drained and
    flaked
1 (4-ounce) jar diced pimiento, drained
2 (1-pound) loaves French bread sliced into ¼"
    slices

Sauté shallots in butter in a Dutch oven until
tender; add flour, stirring until smooth. Cook 1
minute, stirring constantly.

Gradually add milk; cook over medium heat,
stirring constantly, until thickened and bubbly. Stir in
cream and next 5 ingredients. Add crabmeat and
pimiento, stirring until well blended. Cover and
refrigerate up to 24 hours.

To serve, place crabmeat mixture in a large
saucepan. Cook over medium heat until thoroughly
heated, stirring occasionally. Transfer to chafing dish
and keep warm. Serve with French bread slices.
Yield: 6½ cups.

Swiss Vegetable Puffs

½ cup shredded carrots
½ (10-ounce) package frozen chopped spinach,
    thawed and well drained
1 cup (4 ounces) shredded Swiss cheese
1 cup (4 ounces) shredded Cheddar cheese
1 hard-cooked egg, chopped
¼ cup chopped ripe olives
2 tablespoons mayonnaise
1 tablespoon minced onion
¼ teaspoon pepper
Appetizer Puffs (recipe follows)

Place carrots in a small saucepan; add water to
cover. Bring to a boil, reduce heat, and simmer 10
minutes or until tender. Drain and pat dry with
paper towels. Combine carrots, spinach, and next 7
ingredients in a medium bowl, stirring well. Cover
and refrigerate up to 48 hours.

Split puffs; remove and discard soft dough inside.
Fill each cream puff with 1 tablespoon spinach
mixture. Replace tops. Bake at 350° for 12 to 15
minutes or until golden. Yield: 44 appetizers.

Appetizer Puffs:

1⅓ cups water
⅔ cup butter or margarine
¼ teaspoon salt
1⅓ cups all-purpose flour
6 eggs
Vegetable cooking spray

Combine water, butter, and salt in a large saucepan; bring to a boil. Add flour all at once, stirring
vigorously over medium-high heat until mixture
leaves sides of pan and forms a smooth ball. Remove
from heat and cool 10 minutes.

Add eggs, 1 at a time, beating thoroughly with a
wooden spoon after each addition; continue beating
until mixture is smooth.

Drop dough by rounded teaspoonfuls onto cookie
sheets coated with vegetable cooking spray. Bake at
400° for 20 minutes or until lightly browned and
puffed. Cool away from drafts. Freeze in a labeled
airtight container or freezer bag for up to 1 month.
Yield: 44 appetizers.

Pepper-Marinated Olives

6 cups assorted olives (Greek, Italian, Spanish,
    and American)
2 limes, thinly sliced
1 pod fresh garlic, separated into cloves and
    crushed
15 small dried chilies
1 tablespoon freshly ground pepper
4 cups olive oil

Combine olives, limes, garlic, chilies, and pepper
in a large glass container; pour olive oil over mixture,
stirring well. Cover and refrigerate up to 2 months,
stirring occasionally.

Continued on next page.

Let stand at room temperature 1 hour before serving. Remove and discard lime slices. Transfer olive mixture to a serving bowl using a slotted spoon. Reserve remaining olive oil for other uses. Yield: 5 cups.

Chive Dip with Pasta and Vegetable Kabobs

1 (9-ounce) package fresh cheese-filled tortellini
48 small cherry tomatoes
48 (about 1 pound) small fresh broccoli flowerets
1 (8-ounce) package cream cheese, softened
¼ cup milk
2 tablespoons fresh chopped chives
2 tablespoons mayonnaise
2 teaspoons prepared mustard
¼ teaspoon salt
⅛ teaspoon pepper
Fresh chives

Cook pasta according to package directions; drain. Thread pasta, tomatoes, and broccoli alternately on 6" wooden skewers. Set aside.

Combine cream cheese and milk in a small mixing bowl; beat at medium speed of an electric mixer until smooth. Add chives and next 4 ingredients, stirring well. Spoon dip into a bowl and arrange on serving platter along with kabobs. Cover with heavy-duty plastic wrap and refrigerate up to 48 hours.

Just before serving, garnish dip with fresh chives. Yield: 4 dozen.

Tiger Fudge

1 pound white chocolate, chopped
¼ cup plus 1 tablespoon creamy peanut butter, divided
2 (1-ounce) squares semisweet chocolate, chopped

Combine white chocolate and ¼ cup peanut butter in top of a double boiler; bring water to a boil. Reduce heat to low; cook until chocolate melts and mixture is smooth, stirring occasionally. Remove from heat and let stand 15 minutes.

Pour white chocolate mixture into a waxed paper-lined 8"-square pan, spreading evenly; set aside.

Combine semisweet chocolate and remaining 1 tablespoon peanut butter in top of a double boiler; bring water to a boil. Reduce heat to low; cook until chocolate melts and mixture is smooth, stirring occasionally.

Spoon semisweet chocolate mixture into a zip-top plastic bag; remove air and seal. Snip a tiny hole in 1 corner of bag and pipe semisweet chocolate mixture in parallel lines over surface of white chocolate mixture. Pull a wooden pick through lines to create stripes.

Freeze fudge 45 minutes or until firm. Invert and remove pan. Peel off waxed paper. Invert fudge and cut into 1" squares. Place in an airtight container and freeze up to 1 month. Let stand at room temperature 30 minutes before serving. Yield: about 1 pound.

Garlic Cheese Pâté

1 (8-ounce) package cream cheese, softened
2 tablespoons butter or margarine, softened
2 cloves garlic, minced
2 tablespoons finely chopped pimiento
1 tablespoon chopped fresh parsley
½ teaspoon dried whole oregano
¼ teaspoon freshly ground pepper
⅛ teaspoon dried whole thyme
⅛ teaspoon dried whole basil
⅛ teaspoon dried whole dillweed
⅛ teaspoon dried whole marjoram
14 ounces thinly sliced medium-sharp Cheddar cheese, divided
6 ounces thinly sliced Monterey Jack cheese
1 (1-ounce) slice Cheddar cheese
Fresh parsley sprigs
Cherry tomatoes

Combine first 3 ingredients in a medium mixing bowl; beat until light and fluffy. Add pimiento and next 7 ingredients, beating well. Set aside.

Line a 7" springform pan with plastic wrap. Line sides of pan with a third of Cheddar cheese slices. Spread half of cream cheese mixture evenly in bottom of pan; top with half of remaining Cheddar cheese and half of Monterey Jack cheese. Repeat procedure with remaining cream cheese mixture, Cheddar cheese, and Monterey Jack cheese. Cover with plastic wrap and refrigerate for up to 1 week.

Remove pâté from pan and place on serving platter. Let stand at room temperature 1 hour before serving. Using a 2" star-shaped cookie cutter, cut star from 1-ounce Cheddar cheese slice. Place on top of mold. Garnish with parsley and cherry tomatoes. Yield: 6 cups.

Cranberry Gin Spritzers

1 pound fresh cranberries
2½ cups sugar
1 (750-milliliter) bottle gin
10 cups club soda, chilled

Position knife blade in food processor; add cranberries and pulse 3 times or until cranberries are chopped. Combine cranberries and sugar in a large airtight container; pour gin over cranberry mixture, stirring well. Cover and let stand at room temperature 6 weeks, stirring occasionally.

Strain mixture through a cheesecloth-lined colander, extracting 10 cups cranberry juice mixture. Discard chopped cranberries.

Chill cranberry juice mixture. Stir in club soda just before serving. Serve over ice. Yield: 5 quarts.

Spiced Rum Slush

3 cups water
2 cups sugar
8 (3") sticks cinnamon
12 whole cloves
3 cups rum
3 cups orange juice
¾ cup lemon juice
6 cups lemon-lime carbonated beverage, chilled

Combine first 4 ingredients in a medium saucepan; bring to a boil. Reduce heat; simmer, uncovered, 30 minutes. Cool completely; remove and discard cinnamon and cloves. Combine sugar mixture, rum, orange juice, and lemon juice, stirring well. Freeze in an airtight container up to 1 week.

To serve, remove from freezer and let stand 30 minutes. Place frozen mixture in a punch bowl and break into chunks. Add carbonated beverage; stir until slushy. Yield: 14 cups.

Make-Ahead Appetizers

Having friends over during the holidays doesn't have to be a stressful last-minute rush. With careful planning there should be plenty of time to prepare an impressive display of goodies. Getting started weeks in advance will give you time to prepare the appetizers as well as the ambience.

Advance Preparation

🌲 **Six weeks in advance:**
Make Cranberry Gin Spritzer mixture and let stand at room temperature. Make Pepper-Marinated Olives and refrigerate in air-tight container.

🌲 **One month in advance:**
Make and freeze Tiger Fudge.

🌲 **Two weeks in advance:**
Make Appetizer Puffs and freeze in air-tight container.

🌲 **One week in advance:**
Make and freeze Spiced Rum Slush mixture. Make and refrigerate Garlic Cheese Pâté.

🌲 **Two days in advance:**
Make and refrigerate Chive Dip with Pasta and Vegetable Kabobs.

🌲 **One day before:**
Strain and chill Cranberry Gin Spritzer mixture. Make and refrigerate Chesapeake Hot Crab Dip.

🌲 **Morning of:**
Prepare Swiss Vegetable Puff filling. Thaw puffs; fill and bake. Drain Pepper-Marinated Olives, reserving oil for other uses.

Jazz It Up!

Personalize store-bought products like olive oil, vinegar, and preserves with fresh herbs and fine liqueurs.

Specialty Jellies

Here's a way to make "homemade" jelly in a flash. The secret is to start with a jar of purchased jelly or preserves and then add fresh herbs or a liqueur. The result will be a unique combination you can call your own.

For Basil Jelly, melt a 32-ounce jar of apple jelly over low heat in a medium saucepan, stirring occasionally. Remove from heat and stir in two cups of firmly packed fresh basil. Refrigerate 48 hours.

Again melt jelly over low heat in a medium saucepan, stirring occasionally. Strain jelly mixture through a metal sieve, discarding basil. Pour jelly into decorative jars. Seal and store in refrigerator. Yield: three cups.

For Hot Pepper Jelly, substitute two (10-ounce) jars of red currant jelly for apple jelly and one-fourth cup of crushed red pepper for fresh basil. Yield: two and one-third cups.

For Liqueured Strawberry Preserves, melt two cups of strawberry preserves over low heat in a small saucepan, stirring occasionally. Remove from heat and stir in one-third cup of Chambord or other raspberry-flavored liqueur. Spoon mixture into sterilized jars. Cover jars with metal lids and screw on metal bands. Store in refrigerator. Yield: two half-pints.

For Liqueured Peach Preserves, substitute two cups of peach preserves for strawberry preserves and one-third cup of Cognac for Chambord. Yield: two half-pints.

For Liqueured Apricot Preserves, substitute two cups of apricot preserves for strawberry preserves and one-third cup of cream sherry for Chambord. Yield: two half-pints.

Accented Oils

Sprigs of oregano or a cup of crushed red chilies will make a surprising difference in simple vegetable oil. For Herb Oil, combine one cup of fresh basil leaves, one cup of fresh oregano sprigs, both tightly packed, and two cups of vegetable oil in the container of an electric blender; top with cover and process until coarsely chopped. Pour into a one-quart jar; cover with metal lid and screw on band. Let stand in a cool, dark place for one week.

Line a colander or sieve with cheesecloth. Strain mixture, discarding herbs. Pour oil into decorative jars or bottles. Seal with corks or other airtight lids. Store at room temperature. Yield: two cups.

For Citrus Oil, combine three cups of vegetable oil, one-fourth cup plus two tablespoons of grated orange rind (about two oranges), one-fourth cup of grated lime rind (about two limes), and two and one-half tablespoons of grated lemon rind (about two lemons) in a one-quart jar. Continue as for Herb Oil. Yield: three cups.

Left: Grocery shelf jellies will taste like homemade when you heat them and add herbs, hot red peppers, or a special liqueur.

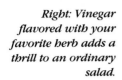

Right: Vinegar flavored with your favorite herb adds a thrill to an ordinary salad.

Left: A sampler of Herb Oil, Citrus Oil, and Chili Pepper Oil makes a quick gift and a nice change of taste. Sauté onions and peppers in Chili Oil for piquant fajitas. Add Herb Oil to boiling water to boost the flavor when cooking pasta. Create a light, pleasing salad dressing by adding rosemary, thyme, and a touch of vinegar to Citrus Oil.

For Chili Pepper Oil, combine one cup of dried red chilies, stems removed, and two cups of vegetable oil in container of electric blender; top with cover and process until chilies are coarsely chopped. Pour into a one-quart jar and continue as for Herb Oil. Yield: two cups.

Fresh Herb Vinegar

Choose fresh basil, dillweed, mint, tarragon, or thyme sprigs to create a flavorful vinegar. Tightly pack one kind of herb in a one-quart jar. Add enough vinegar to cover herb sprigs. Cover with metal lid and screw on band. Let stand in a bright place for three weeks.

Strain vinegar, discarding herbs. Pour herb vinegar into decorative jar or bottle. Place fresh sprigs of

appropriate herb in vinegar to indicate flavor. Seal with cork or other airtight lid. Store at room temperature. Yield: about three cups.

Pleasures of the Season

Simple Pleasures

Joan Vibert compares her family's Christmas tree to a fine old quilt. Just as a handmade quilt may spur a memory—scraps from a child's pastel dress worn years ago or floral curtains from another time— each ornament on the tree carries a reminder of the year it was made. This is because the Vibert family members have created all their tree's ornaments.

From the start, Joan and her husband, Jim, wanted to make family celebrations special for his three daughters and her two daughters and two sons. On their first Christmas, the combined family of nine gathered to make stockings and ornaments for all.

Now, every year the family adds more decorations for the holidays. At these family craft fests, memories as well as ornaments are made.

"You don't need to throw out a lot of money to start a tradition," Joan says assuredly. "Traditions are created with emotions and by doing things for others and with others."

This is a lesson the Viberts hope to pass on to their children and grandchildren. "Christmas was so important to me as a child, and I want it to be for my children and grandchildren," Joan says.

Joan shares a childhood memory when telling of last year's Christmas project that involved her admitted weakness: pearl buttons.

"To keep me out of trouble, my grandmother would sit me down on her bed to make button necklaces from her button collection," Joan recalls. "Whenever I see pearl buttons, I think of her."

Combining this love of buttons with holiday decorating, Joan suggested that the family make button garlands for their Christmas tree. Her daughter Kristy, who had never been much interested in crafts, was home from college for the holidays. She agreed to help her mother make the garlands for the tree. Tying button after button together with string, they soon had draped graceful garlands all over the kitchen. By the time bedtime rolled around, Joan was exhausted, but Kristy was hooked. She sent Joan off to bed, promising to follow after making "just one more garland."

Even with such a large family to inspire, Joan says that she and Jim always find the energy for the holidays. "We realize that these are the years when childhood memories are being created," Joan says. "The simple pleasures, like a plate of freshly baked and decorated cookies, make the most lasting impressions."

Above: Joan, a craft designer by trade, created this eagle she named Grover. He was inspired by snow eagles atop roofs in Lancaster, Pennsylvania, where they hold snow in place for winter insulation. (Joan shares her instructions for making Grover on page 50.)

Above: A tiny example of the family's pearl button garland drapes a miniature tree. Joan purchased the celluloid reindeer because they reminded her of deer in the Christmas village scenes her grandmother had.

Above: Joan, with her eldest grandson, Duncan, surveys what she calls the family's "living history tree."

Right: Joan designed and stitched this appliqué and embroidery interpretation of a primitive painting by Joseph Whiting.

109

Above: Stitching these stars and gingerbread men and women can be a memory-making family project.

Cookie Cutter Ornaments

These cookie cutter ornaments are a great way for children to learn sewing skills. With a little guidance, kids will soon be able to complete an ornament on their own.

Materials for 1 gingerbread man or woman and 1 star:
patterns on page 153
tracing paper
water-soluble marker
2 (6" x 8") pieces of red fabric for gingerbread man or woman
2 (4") squares of Christmas print for star
embroidery floss: black or white
5 (¼") black buttons
crewel needle
pearl cotton: white, red
polyester stuffing
pinking shears

For gingerbread man or woman, use tracing paper and water-soluble marker to transfer pattern to right side of 1 piece of fabric. Do not cut out.

Referring to pattern for placement and using 2 strands of black or white embroidery floss, sew on buttons for eyes. If desired, embroider mouth with small running stitches and sew buttons on clothes.

With wrong sides facing and raw edges aligned, pin fabric pieces together. Using 1 strand of white pearl cotton, take small running stitches around body along traced outline, leaving small opening on side for stuffing. Do not clip thread.

Firmly stuff gingerbread person. Continue stitching to close opening. Secure and clip threads. Using pinking shears, cut around gingerbread person, ¼" from stitching line.

For hanger, thread needle with a 6" length of red pearl cotton and stitch through top back of head. Knot ends together to form a loop.

For star, substitute Christmas print for red fabric and finish as for gingerbread ornament, omitting embroidery details.

For garland, stitch desired number of each ornament and then pin stars and gingerbread people alternately to a length of ribbon (see photograph).

110

Horsing Around!

The first Christmas began in a simple stable used to shelter farm animals. There's no doubt the barn deserves a touch of holiday atmosphere.

When choosing materials for decorating a stable or barn, remember what the animals like and dislike. For a horse's wreath like the one in the photograph, choose all-time favorites like stalks of oats, bunches of baby carrots, and juicy red apples.

Start with a purchased evergreen wreath; then anchor oat stalks through the wreath base. Tie bundles of carrots onto the wreath with raffia. Using florists' picks, attach the apples to the wreath in clusters. (Be sure to remove all of the florists' picks before sharing the apples with your horse.)

Wrap a soft burlap-style ribbon around the wreath to add another splash of red. Enhance the rustic look with assorted twigs.

Use your common sense when choosing decorating materials. Remember your horse's health as well as its preferences. Watch out for mold on the hay; beware of rotting spots on the fruit. Stay away from any poisonous greenery such as mistletoe.

Considering your horse's appetite when making the wreath will pay off as a belated Christmas treat when you dismantle the wreath and hand out a nibble of oats.

Below: In addition to the huge wreath, swags of fir drape gracefully over the stalls. Bundles of large and small carrots tied with raffia accent the garland.

Teddy Bear Tea Party

"I won't collect anything that's not lighthearted and fun," says Sandy Gilliam. Among Sandy's many heart-warming collections are teddy bears that she collected with her daughter, Carrie. Each bear was so special that Sandy and Carrie adopted it into the family and gave it its own name. The teddy bear collection numbers between 70 and 80 and includes both new and antique bears. All year long, they are kept on display in almost every room of Sandy's home in Roswell, Georgia, for family and friends to enjoy.

This year, Sandy and Questers, an antiques study group, have planned a teddy bear tea as a fund-raiser for the historic Bulloch Hall Museum in Roswell. Antebellum Bulloch Hall was the family home of Martha "Mittie" Bulloch, who married Theodore Roosevelt, Sr., three days before Christmas in 1853. They moved to New York City and later became the parents of President Theodore "Teddy" Roosevelt. The tea party at Bulloch Hall will celebrate the president's October birthday.

The teddy bear was so named because President

Above: Besides teddy bears, craftswoman and collector Sandy Gilliam collects, among other things, Santas, Adam and Eves, and Noah's arks. Her prized collections fill every corner of her home. She wants her friends to enjoy them, too, and does not believe collections should be locked up behind glass. Her pieces, even the rare collectibles, are out in full view, seeming to say, "Please do touch."

Roosevelt, on a hunting trip, refused to shoot a trapped female bear. A political cartoonist called the bear "Teddy's Bear." Later a toy bear handmade by a toy shop owner attracted much attention, and the shop owner began to manufacture "teddy" bears. They became an instant success and have remained perennially popular.

During the Christmas season, Sandy especially enjoys her bear collection. Soon after Thanksgiving, she selects up to a dozen bears to gather around her breakfast room table for an annual holiday teddy bear tea party. This tea party is part of the entertainment for her annual open house each December. Granny, an almost-life-sized soft-sculpture doll by Tennessee artist Sara Baker, is always invited to the party. "The bears couldn't do without her," says Sandy.

To accompany the teddy bear party, Sandy creates a story about the bears and their guests that she relates to her friends, who enjoy the fantasy as much as she does. The bears recently discussed whether one of the group should dress as President Teddy Roosevelt for the celebration of the president's birthday at Bulloch Hall.

Will one of Sandy's bears come dressed as President Roosevelt? The bears have sworn to keep it a secret until the day of the Bulloch Hall tea party.

Above: The bears enjoy a visit from a Teddy Roosevelt doll crafted by artist Evelyn Nesbitt of England.

Left: Visitors who come upon soft-sculpture Granny for the first time are taken aback by the realism effected by Tennessee artist Sara Baker. Granny always comes to Sandy's annual teddy bear tea party and serves as the bears' confidante.

Below: Bear friends gather around the table and chat with Granny about the upcoming celebration of President Theodore "Teddy" Roosevelt's birthday. They eagerly await their tea and crumpets.

Snowy Hat and Muffler

Bright blue and creamy white wool yarns combine to create a "snow-at-night" effect on this knitted hat and muffler.

Materials:
chart on page 153
worsted-weight wool (220-yard skein): 2 skeins blue, 2 skeins white
size G crochet hook (optional)
4 (size 7) double-pointed knitting needles, or size to obtain gauge
stitch markers
stitch holder
size 7 (16"-long) circular knitting needle, or size to obtain gauge
stuffing
5" square of cardboard

SIZES: Scarf is 51" long. Directions for hat are for size 4-6 years (17½" circumference). Changes for size 7-10 years (19" circumference) are in parentheses.

GAUGE: 5 sts and 6 rows = 1" in St st.

Note: Knitting Abbreviations are on page 153. The following directions use an invisible cast-on. If a normal cast-on is used instead, carefully sew ends of scarf to prevent flaring at edges. The rolled brim of the hat can be stuffed and sewn after all knitting is completed, if desired.

To change colors, wrap old yarn over new so that no holes occur. Carry color not in use loosely across back of work. To prevent a ridge of stretched sts when working on dpn, move 1 or 2 sts from each needle to the next every few rnds. Move the same number of sts in the same direction each time.

SCARF: To make invisible cast-on, with size G crochet hook and scrap yarn, chain 55 loosely. Cut yarn and draw end loosely through last chain. Insert 1 dpn through the bump at the back of the 2nd or 3rd chain from the last chain made, and draw through a loop of white yarn. Continue along chain, drawing a loop of white through each of the next 47 chains for a total of 48 sts. Arrange the sts on 3 dpn. Slip a marker on needle after last st to indicate beg of rnd.

Connect and k in the rnd. K 20 rnds with white. Work next 25 rnds according to chart, rep indicated portion of design for pat. Work rows 18-25 of chart once more. With blue, work even until piece measures 42" from beg.

Turn chart upside down and work rows 1-8. Then work rows 1-25 of chart. K 21 rnds with white. Place sts on holder.

FINISHING: Fold end of scarf so that 3 motifs are centered on each side. Remove waste chain from cast-on edge and arrange sts on 2 dpn (24 sts on each needle). Graft sts tog. Rep for other end of scarf.

HAT: Work invisible cast-on as for scarf, but chain 95 (102). With circular needle, draw up 88 (96) loops of white through back bumps of chain. Slip a marker on needle after last st to indicate beg of rnd.

Connect and k in the rnd. K 26 (28) rnds with white.

Rolled brim: Turn up cast-on edge with purl side out. Undo end of chain and carefully pull until first k st is free. Place this k st on a dpn with the right edge of the st close to you and the left edge of the st at the far side of the needle. Continue freeing k sts and placing them on the dpn. When there are approximately 20 sts on the needle, work them into the body of the hat as follows: Holding dpn parallel to and in front of circular needle, insert tip of the other end of circular needle into first st on dpn and into first st on circular needle. K these 2 sts tog. Continue to k 2 sts tog (1 from dpn and 1 from circular needle) around, stuffing brim as you work around. When brim is completed, k 1 rnd with white.

Work rows 1-23 of chart (rows 1-25 for larger size), rep indicated portion of design for pat. K 1 (2) rnd even with blue. * K 1, k 2 tog, k 3, ssk, rep from * around. K 3 rnds even. * K 1, k 2 tog, k 1, ssk, rep from * around. K 3 rnds even. K 1, sl 2 sts k-wise, k 1, pass both sl sts over, rep from * around. K 3 rnds even. K 2 tog around. K 1 rnd even. Thread yarn through rem sts, pull tightly to gather, and secure yarn.

FINISHING: To make pom-pom, wind white yarn around 5" square of cardboard 100 times. Cut strands at top and bottom. Tie a piece of yarn tightly around middle of strands. Trim ends even. Tack to top of hat.

Right: Bundle up your boys in these snowy accessories before sending them outside on a winter afternoon.

Combine first 5 ingredients in a medium bowl; stir well. Spoon batter into paper-lined muffin pans, filling two-thirds full. Bake at 350° for 20 minutes or until a wooden pick inserted in center comes out clean. Remove from pans and cool on wire racks.

Melt raspberry preserves in a small saucepan over low heat. Make an indentation in the center of each tart, using handle of wooden spoon. Spoon ½ teaspoon of melted preserves into each indentation.

Spoon melted chocolate into a zip-top plastic bag; remove air and seal plastic bag. Snip a tiny hole in 1 corner of bag and pipe chocolate over tarts. Top with toasted almond slices. Yield: 1½ dozen.

Butterscotch Oat Bars

1 (21½-ounce) package fudge brownie mix
1 cup quick-cooking oats, uncooked
⅓ cup butter or margarine, softened
1 (8-ounce) package cream cheese, softened
1 (3-ounce) package cream cheese, softened
2 eggs
½ cup commercial butterscotch ice cream topping
½ cup chopped pecans
3 (1-ounce) squares semisweet chocolate, melted and cooled

Combine first 3 ingredients in a medium mixing bowl. Beat at low speed of an electric mixer until crumbly. Press mixture into a greased 13" x 9" x 2" baking pan. Bake at 350° for 15 minutes. Cool slightly.

Combine cream cheese, eggs, and butterscotch topping in a medium bowl. Beat at medium speed of an electric mixer until smooth. Stir in chopped pecans. Spread cream cheese mixture over brownie mixture. Bake at 350° for an additional 15 minutes. Cool completely and cut into 2 dozen bars.

Spoon melted chocolate into a zip-top plastic bag; remove air and seal plastic bag. Snip a tiny hole in 1 corner of zip-top bag and pipe chocolate onto bars. Yield: 2 dozen.

Quick-Mix Treats

These quick-mix recipes allow you to "fudge" a little when you don't have the time to bake holiday goodies from scratch. Each recipe begins with a purchased fudge brownie mix that you dress up with fruits, candies, or nuts so that even the most discerning palate won't be able to guess your secret!

Linzer Tarts

1 (21½-ounce) package fudge brownie mix
½ cup water
½ cup vegetable oil
2 eggs
½ teaspoon almond extract
¼ cup raspberry preserves
4 (1-ounce) squares semisweet chocolate, melted and cooled
Sliced almonds, toasted

116

Left: One bite of these miniature, sugar-frosted "fruits" will prove they're just as delicious as they are exquisite.

Sugar Fruit Tea Cookies

The realistic detail of these Fruit Tea Cookies may lead you to believe that only a skilled baker will be able to make them. On the contrary, the cookie halves are simply baked and then joined with buttercream filling. Tinted sugar and a mint-leaf garnish finish their appearance.

Ingredients:
1 cup butter, softened
1 cup sugar
2 eggs
¼ cup milk
½ teaspoon almond extract
3½ cups all-purpose flour, divided
Buttercream Filling (recipe follows)
Tinted Sugars (recipe follows)
Whole cloves
Fresh mint leaves (optional)

Cream butter; gradually add sugar, beating until light and fluffy. Add eggs, milk, and almond extract, beating well. Add 2 cups of flour, beating until smooth. Stir in remaining 1½ cups flour, using a wooden spoon.

Shape dough into 1" balls and place 2" apart on ungreased baking sheets. Bake at 350° for 10 minutes or just until bottoms of cookies are lightly browned. Cool on wire racks.

Spread ¼ teaspoon Buttercream Filling on flat side of 1 cookie. Place the flat side of a second cookie on top of filling, pressing gently. Repeat procedure with remaining cookies and filling.

Using a small paintbrush, coat each cookie lightly with water. Roll each cookie in color of tinted sugar desired. Let cookies stand for 15 minutes.

Press a whole clove in seam at top of each cookie for "stem." Garnish with mint leaves, if desired. Yield: about 3 dozen.

Buttercream Filling:

⅓ cup butter, softened
1 cup sifted powdered sugar
1 teaspoon orange juice
⅛ teaspoon vanilla extract

Cream butter; gradually add sugar, beating until light and fluffy. Add orange juice and vanilla; beat well. Yield: ¾ cup.

Tinted Sugars:

Orange cookies: Combine ⅓ cup sugar, 7 drops yellow food coloring, and 4 drops red food coloring; stir well. Yield: ⅓ cup.

Peach cookies: Combine ⅓ cup sugar, 3 drops yellow food coloring, and 2 drops red food coloring; stir well. Yield ⅓ cup.

Apple cookies: Combine ⅓ cup sugar and 8 drops red food coloring; stir well. Yield: ⅓ cup.

Yo-yos Take a Spin on Tradition

Ornaments, garlands, and even fancy collars are the rewarding results when you stitch these simple yo-yos together. Just cut circles of Christmassy fabric, gather the edges together with a quick running stitch, and then tack the gathered circles together.

Yo-yo Ornament

Materials for 1 ornament:
scrap of Christmassy calico or red pindot fabric
thread to match fabric
2 (7") pieces of ⅛"-wide satin ribbon

Cut 1 (6½") circle from fabric. Turn under edge of circle ¼". Make running stitches around circle through both layers. Pull thread tightly, gathering edges to center, and tie off thread to secure. With opening centered (see Diagram 1), spread gathers evenly and press circles flat.

For hanger, fold 1 piece of ribbon in half to form a loop and tack to back of ornament. Tie remaining ribbon in a bow and tack to front of ornament at bottom of loop.

Yo-yo Garland

Materials:
scraps of Christmassy calico and red pindot fabric
threads to match fabrics

Cut 29 (4½") circles from fabrics of the type listed.

Referring to instructions for yo-yo ornament, make 29 yo-yos.

Turn flat sides up and, referring to photograph, tack yo-yos together at sides in a single row to form a garland.

Yo-yo Wreath Ornament

Materials for 1 ornament:
scraps of Christmassy calico and red pindot fabric
threads to match fabrics
polyester stuffing
14" (⅛"-wide) white ribbon

Cut 16 (4½") circles from fabric.

Refer to instructions for yo-yo ornament to make 16 yo-yos, adding a small amount of stuffing to inside of each yo-yo before gathering.

With gathered sides of yo-yos facing in same direction and using a double strand of matching thread, string yo-yos together through centers. Bring ends of thread together to form a circle and knot thread.

For hanger, pull ribbon through hole in ornament, loop, and tie ends into a bow.

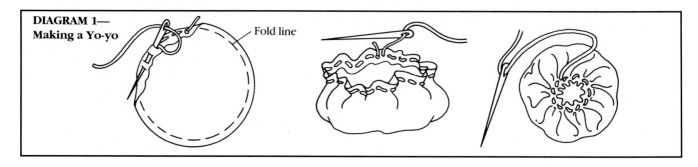

DIAGRAM 1—
Making a Yo-yo
Fold line

Diamond Collar

Materials:
¾ yard (45"-wide) white brocade or taffeta
thread to match fabric
3 hooks and eyes

Note: Finished size of collar is 18" square.

Cut 72 (4½") circles from fabric. Referring to instructions for yo-yo ornament, make 72 yo-yos.

Turn flat sides up. Tack the yo-yos together at sides to make 6 rows of 9 yo-yos each, and 6 rows of 3 yo-yos each.

Referring to Diagram 2 for placement, tack yo-yo rows together, leaving open where indicated.

Finish collar by sewing hooks and eyes at opening.

Round Collar

Materials:
½ yard (45"-wide) white brocade or taffeta
thread to match fabric
1 hook and eye

Note: Finished size is 14" circle.

Cut 29 (4½") circles from fabric. Referring to instructions for yo-yo ornament, make 29 yo-yos.

Turn flat sides up and, referring to photograph and Diagram 3 for placement, tack yo-yos together at sides, leaving opening where indicated.

Finish collar by sewing hook and eye at opening.

Above: These hand-crafted collars reminiscent of yesteryear are simply yo-yos tacked together in a diamond or circular pattern. White brocade and taffeta yo-yos make these elegant accessories, but you can make seasonal sensations by stitching them in bright reds and greens.

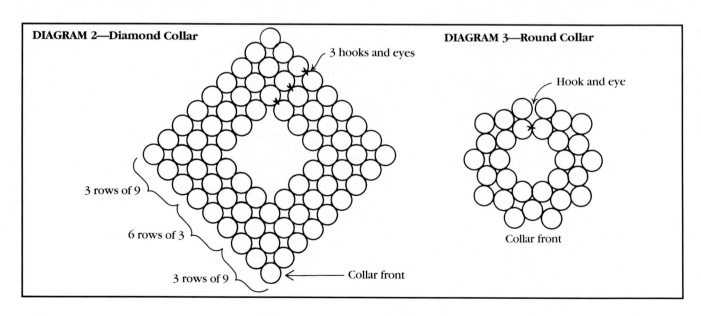

DIAGRAM 2—Diamond Collar

3 hooks and eyes

3 rows of 9

6 rows of 3

3 rows of 9

Collar front

DIAGRAM 3—Round Collar

Hook and eye

Collar front

Childhood Sweets

Although we had kids in mind when we chose these recipes, we know that adults will enjoy making and eating these scrumptious treats, too! Popcorn balls and taffy are old-time favorites, but since the mixtures must be cooked at high temperatures, an adult should supervise the cooking of these goodies.

Grandma's Honey Taffy

1 cup sugar
½ cup water
⅓ cup honey
⅛ teaspoon salt
1 teaspoon vanilla extract
Red or green food coloring (optional)

Combine first 4 ingredients in a small Dutch oven; cook over low heat, stirring gently, until sugar dissolves. Cover and cook over medium heat 2 to 3 minutes to dissolve any sugar crystals from sides of pan. Uncover and cook on medium heat, without stirring, until mixture reaches soft crack stage (280°). Remove from heat; stir in vanilla. Add food coloring, if desired.

Pour candy onto an oiled 15" x 10" x 1" jellyroll pan or marble slab. Let cool to touch; oil hands and pull candy just until mixture becomes elastic. (Candy can be divided into portions at this point to begin pulling.) Continue pulling candy until light in color and difficult to pull. Pull candy into a rope, ½" in diameter. Cut into 1" pieces or shape into desired designs. Wrap candy in waxed paper. Yield: ½ pound.

Ooey Gooey Popcorn Balls

2 quarts popped popcorn
½ cup chopped roasted peanuts
⅔ cup firmly packed brown sugar
¼ cup light corn syrup
¼ cup water
⅛ teaspoon salt
2½ tablespoons butter or margarine
¼ teaspoon vanilla extract
1 cup candy-coated milk chocolate pieces

Combine popcorn and peanuts in a large bowl; toss gently and set aside.

Combine sugar, corn syrup, water, and salt in a medium saucepan; cook over low heat until sugar dissolves, stirring gently.

Cover and cook over medium heat 2 to 3 minutes to dissolve any sugar crystals from sides of pan. Uncover and cook over medium heat, without stirring, to hard-ball stage (254°). Remove from heat; stir in butter and vanilla.

Pour hot syrup evenly over popcorn mixture, stirring well with a wooden spoon. Let cool slightly; stir in candy pieces.

Oil hands and shape mixture into 3" balls. Place balls on waxed paper to dry. Wrap balls individually in plastic wrap, and store them in a cool, dry place. Yield: 1 dozen.

Cedarburg's Christmas Bazaar

Creativity leads some people down unimagined paths. Just ask the co-directors of "Christmas in the Country," a successful annual craft show in Cedarburg, Wisconsin. They describe their humble and hurried beginnings fondly, but it's clear that 17 years ago they never envisioned that they were developing such a long-lived, grand-scale event.

In 1974, artists Susan Hale, Luella Doss, and Sandra Pape got together weekly with a few friends for artistic inspiration. They shared ideas and discussed new projects while their children played. When the group attended a small Christmas craft show in nearby Milwaukee, they returned convinced that they, too, could produce such a show, maybe a better one. They didn't let anything dissuade them, not even the fact that they had only two weeks to get ready for the event.

In a flurry they made hundreds of ornaments, dolls, wreaths, wooden toys, and jams and jellies. Susan's husband had converted an old fieldstone summer kitchen behind their house into a weaving studio for her. This became the perfect country setting for their handmade wares. Christmas trees were decked with ornaments. Weavings and quilts hung from the beams. Santas, flying angels, and furry lambs lined the shelves. Spiced tea and cookies waited for visitors.

For the next five years they held the show annually at the little stone cottage. But their continued success made it plain that a larger site was needed. They all wanted to find a place that had the same warm atmosphere as Susan's studio.

Sandra's husband had recently purchased a historic winery in Cedarburg. With its stone walls and multi-leveled wooden floors, the old building overlooking Cedar Creek was ideal.

Amid huge wine barrels, the Christmas folk-and-fine-art show has grown into a year-round business for Susan, Luella, Sandra, and now Veronica Hammes as well.

There are numerous reasons for their success. One is the group's continued commitment to creativity. The number one goal of the show is to encourage originality in the exhibitors, who now total more than 50. Every year, one third of the inventory of each artisan must be new material. This keeps the creative juices flowing and offers shoppers unique items.

Sharing and cooperating are also cornerstones of the show. A bond has formed not only between the directors, but also among the exhibitors. This show requires a real commitment of time, especially for the artists with families. With all the work called for in this four-day show, camaraderie is often what keeps everyone going. This affinity mixed with a great appreciation for one another's work results in a good bit of trading among the exhibitors themselves!

The good-natured admiration spills over to the families. On Saturday evening of the show, spouses are honored at a "Gentleman in the Country" dinner where husbands have a chance to "roast" their wives. The kids are included in the show with a "Children's Corner" where they sell their own wares.

Luella explains the show's success: "It's a combination of hospitality and goodwill with an explosion of creativity and a fantasy of nostalgia."

Opposite top: "Christmas in the Country" co-directors (left to right) Susan Hale, Sandra Pape, Luella Doss, and Veronica Hammes gather around one of several community trees. When the show moved to the winery, the group decided they needed a way to identify themselves. Handmade personalized aprons were the answer.

122

Left: The Cedar Creek Settlement Winery is transformed into a Christmas fantasy the first weekend of every December.

123

Carving a New Career

When Charlie Royston walked into an antiques store a few years ago, an old pocketknife caught his eye. Little did Charlie know when he bought the knife that it would lead him into a new career.

Charlie's wife, Boots, owns an antiques and folk art shop in Roswell, Georgia. She encouraged Charlie, a construction materials salesman, to use his newly acquired knife and his spare time to try carving some simple two-dimensional Santa Clauses for her shop. What started as a hobby for Charlie gradually turned into a career in folk art carving, as he became more and more fascinated with what he could do with his hands and his knife. "I began to round out the flat Santas," says Charlie. "I carved a little more and a little more and found that I could create a three-dimensional Santa."

Charlie began to study old-fashioned Santa carvings while continuing to perfect his own carving skills. A significant milestone came for him in 1984, when he carved a figure that he calls his first "real" Santa—one that satisfied his artistic goals. Fine detail became one of his hallmarks. His many carvings include a Nativity, Shakers, and a reproduction of an 1870s Noah's Ark. His most recent work is a Civil War chess set, with carved likenesses of Abraham Lincoln and Jefferson Davis.

In just a few years, Charlie has gained a reputation for extraordinary carved pieces. The Museum of American Folk Art in New York City, the National Archives in Washington, D.C., and the Museum Store in Deerfield, Massachusetts, feature his work.

Charlie wants his art to be affordable, so Boots suggested that he make copies for people to buy. Now Charlie makes molds from his originals so that he can cast replicas in a wood resin composition.

Charlie has never had an art or carving course and vows that he'll never take one. "If I do, I'll start carving like someone else, not myself," he says.

Above: Their arms still loaded with gifts, these Santas take a moment to rest a bit before continuing rounds on a busy Christmas Eve.

Right: This striking display of Charlie Royston's Santas immediately captures the attention of anyone who walks into the Concord House in Roswell, Georgia. Santa fanciers can choose from a fine array of folk Santas to add to their own collections.

124

Left: One can almost reach back in time and hear these realistically carved carolers singing, "Here we come a-wassailing . . ."

Below: Charlie Royston, Georgia folk artist, uses his imagination and the deft touch of his carving knife to give each Santa its own personality. His carvings have been featured in several national magazines and in the Smithsonian catalog. He also enjoys collecting Santa candy containers, like the large Santa in the center.

Ideas

Candy Canes Add a New Twist

With the large variety of candy canes and other sweet treats available, you can easily transform your surroundings into a magical candyland this Christmas. One bit of advice: Buy extra supplies. Somehow they seem to "disappear" quickly!

Cottage of Sweets

First, use your hot-glue gun to glue straight candy sticks together for the four walls. For the front and back walls, cut additional sticks in declining lengths and glue in place to form the high peaks. (You may find that the best way to cut the sticks is by biting them—yum, an added treat!) Glue posterboard supports to the front and back walls for extra support. After gluing the walls together, make a posterboard roof and glue to the top of the walls. Glue candy canes to the roof and hard candies to the

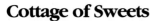

Above: For this peppermint confection, hot-glue the ends of two large candy canes together to form a heart. Glue a peppermint candy to the end of a short length of ribbon. Dangle the candy from the center of the heart by wrapping the ribbon around the canes and gluing it to secure. Glue a ribbon hanger to the back of the heart and a bow to the front.

walls and roof for windows, door, and chimney (see photograph). Glue the completed house to a white cardboard base. For the fence, glue two small candy stick crossrails to one small candy cane fence post and repeat to make enough to enclose the house. Glue fence posts and stepping stones to the cardboard base. Artificial snow sprinkled over the entire house adds a touch of enchantment. *Note:* For information on ordering the candy canes seen on these pages, see the source listing on page 154.

Left: This charming candy cottage is constructed by using your hot-glue gun and as many varieties of candy canes, sticks, and hard candies as you can find.

Right: Candy canes transform this antique drying rack into a playful Christmas creation.

Below: Want to take a thoughtful gift to the hostess who has everything? Simply drape candy canes over the edge of a purchased plant and secure them with a polka-dot bow.

Right: To quickly spruce up a package, just add a candy cane or two. For the starburst, hot-glue the ends of two small candy canes together to form a heart. Repeat to make four hearts; then glue hearts together at the center. Adorn with a bow.

Patterns

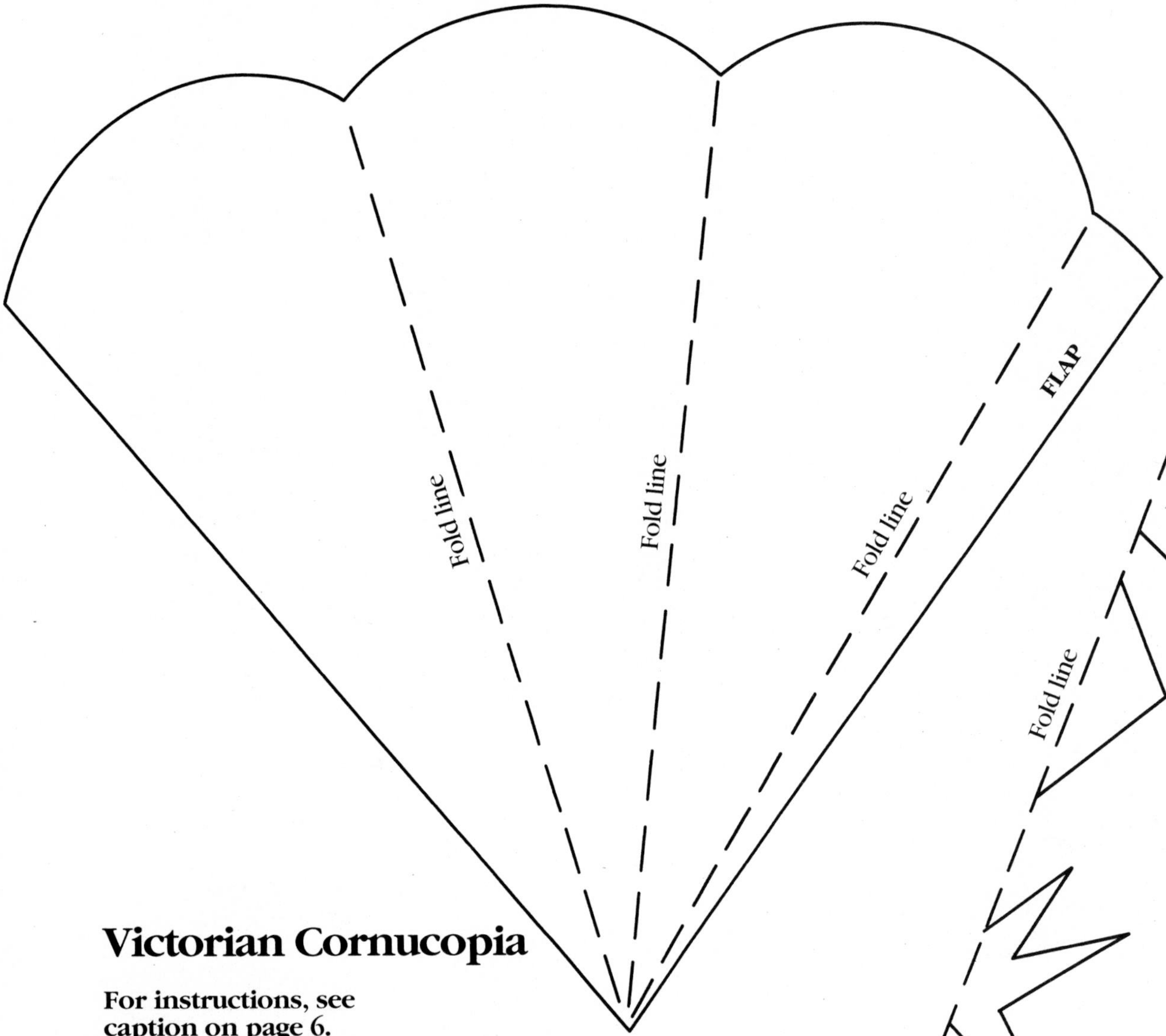

Fold line

Fold line

Fold line

FLAP

Fold line

Victorian Cornucopia

For instructions, see
caption on page 6.
Pattern is full-size.

Snowflake Table Covering

Instructions are on page 20.
Enlarge pattern to twice
its size on copy machine.

Cutting line

Hole placement

Christmas Holly Table Runner

Instructions are on page 19.
Pattern is full-size.

Continue couching
around outer border.

2

2

2

1

1

1

1

1

1

French knot placement

1

3

3

2

3

2

3

3

3

3

2

1

3

3

Outline stitch

3

3

3

Farmyard Fence

Instructions are on page 20.
Pattern is full-size.

3

3

3

3

3

3

3

Couching stitch

Overlapping end

Note: Numbers are for DMC floss. Using 3 strands of floss, outline-stitch berries in 814 Garnet-dark, leaves in 3364 Pine Green, and border detail in 726 Topaz-light. Couch-stitch outer border, using 3 strands of 726 Topaz-light over 12 strands of 780 Topaz-dark. Work French knots, using 3 strands of 783 Christmas Yellow.

Color Key for Paints
1 Red
2 Green
3 Gold

Overlapping end

Repeat pattern until fence is desired length.

Noel Door Banner

Instructions are on page 11.
Each square equals 1".
Patterns include ¼" seam allowances.

LETTER N
Cut 1 from red fabric.

LETTER O
Cut 1 from red fabric.

Overlap
O here.

Overlap
E here.

Country Newspaper Border

Instructions are on page 21.
Pattern is full-size.

Place on fold.

Hole placement

Hole placement

Cut out heart and bottom scallop; then unfold once
and cut out house and tree.

Place on fold.

Place on fold.

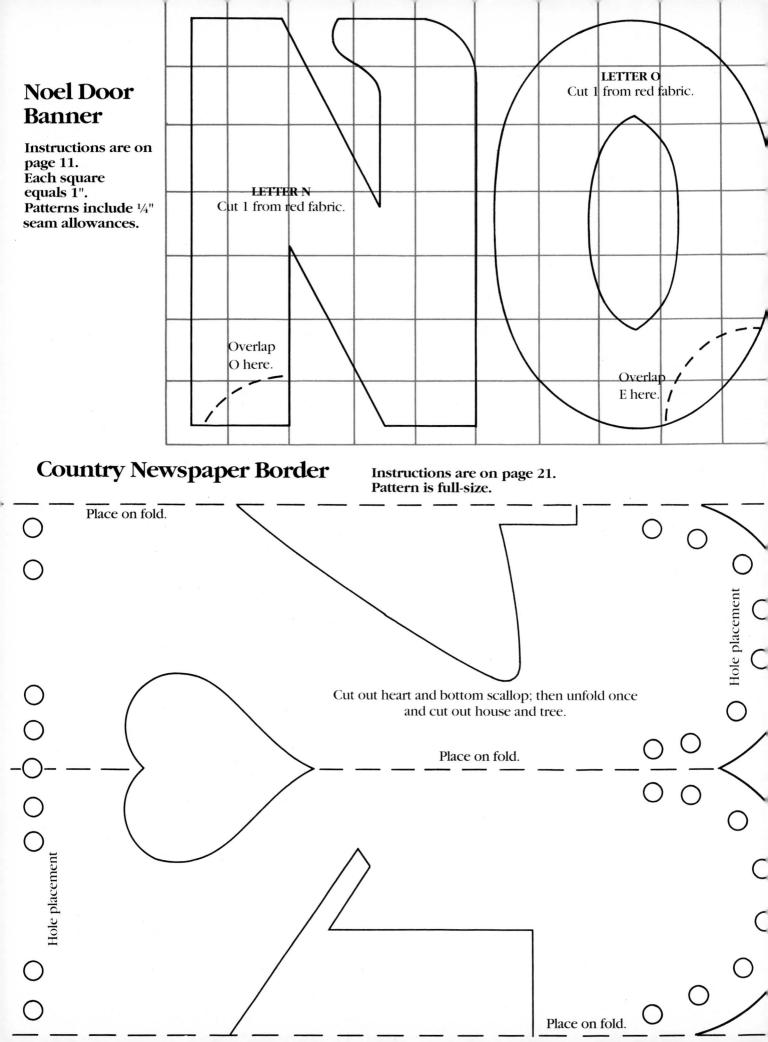

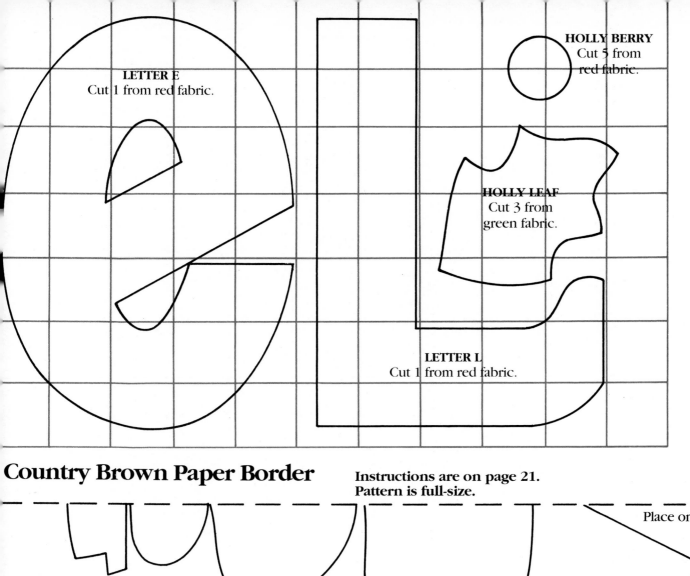

LETTER E
Cut 1 from red fabric.

HOLLY BERRY
Cut 5 from red fabric.

HOLLY LEAF
Cut 3 from green fabric.

LETTER L
Cut 1 from red fabric.

Country Brown Paper Border

**Instructions are on page 21.
Pattern is full-size.**

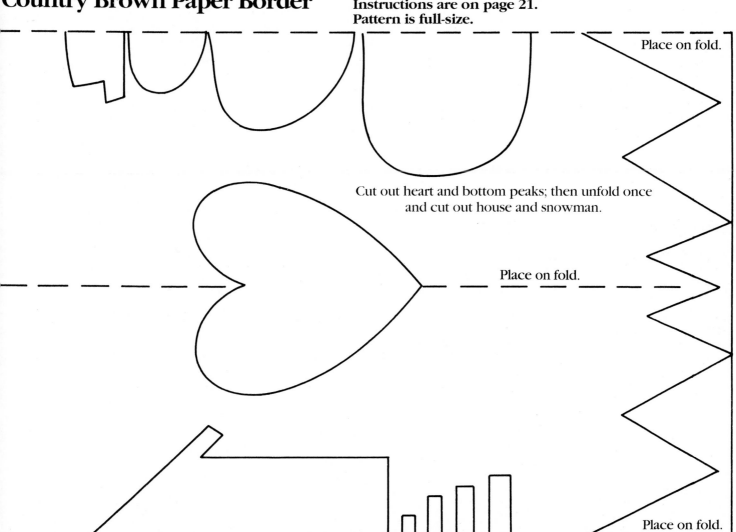

Place on fold.

Cut out heart and bottom peaks; then unfold once
and cut out house and snowman.

Place on fold.

Place on fold.

Snow Cowboy

**Instructions are on page 25.
Patterns are full-size.**

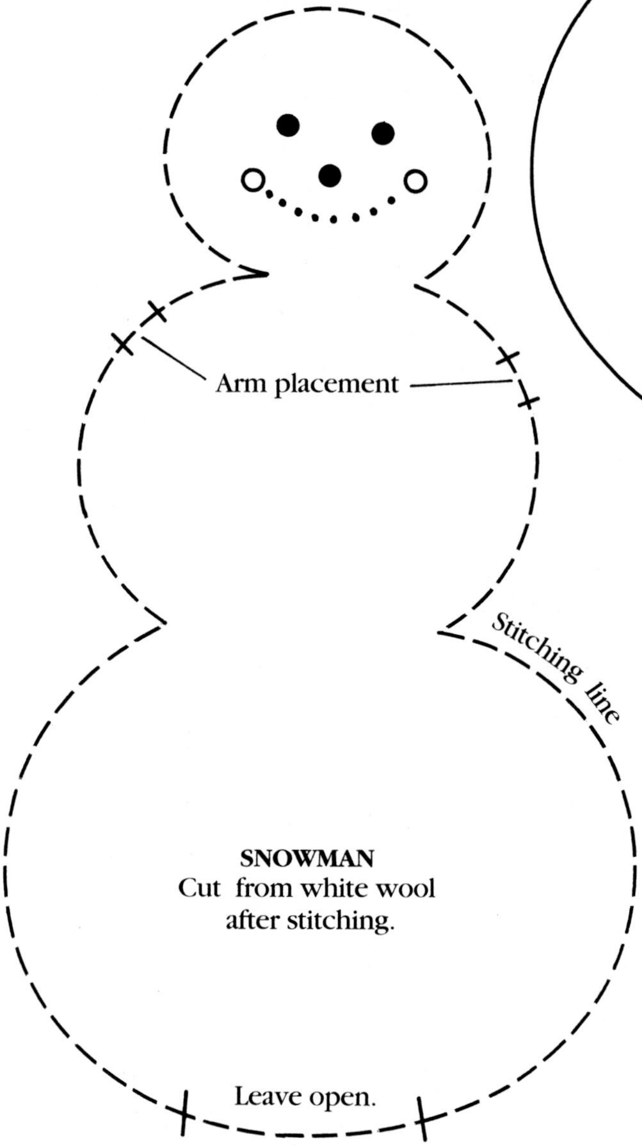

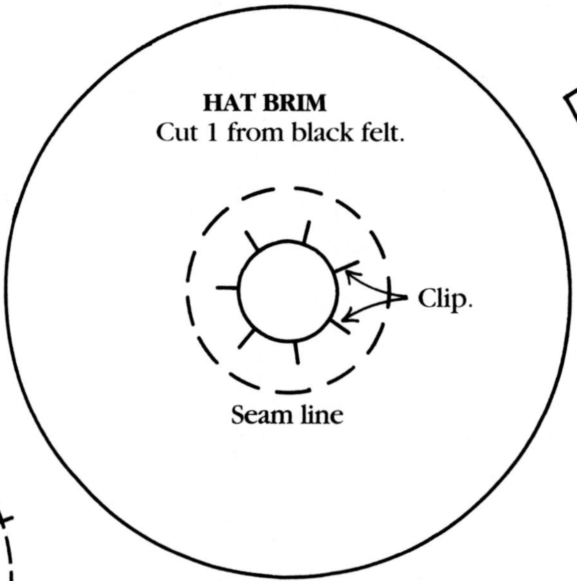

HAT BRIM
Cut 1 from black felt.

Clip.

Seam line

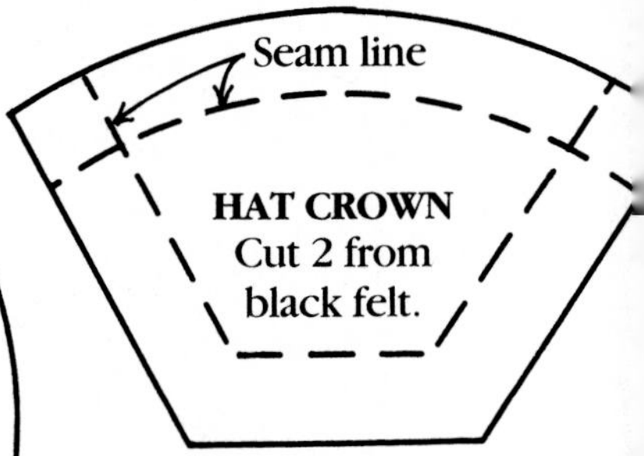

Seam line

HAT CROWN
Cut 2 from
black felt.

**Hat patterns include
¼" seam allowances.**

Arm placement

Stitching line

SNOWMAN
Cut from white wool
after stitching.

Leave open.

Cozy Christmas Cabin

**Instructions are on
page 26.
Pattern is
full-size.**

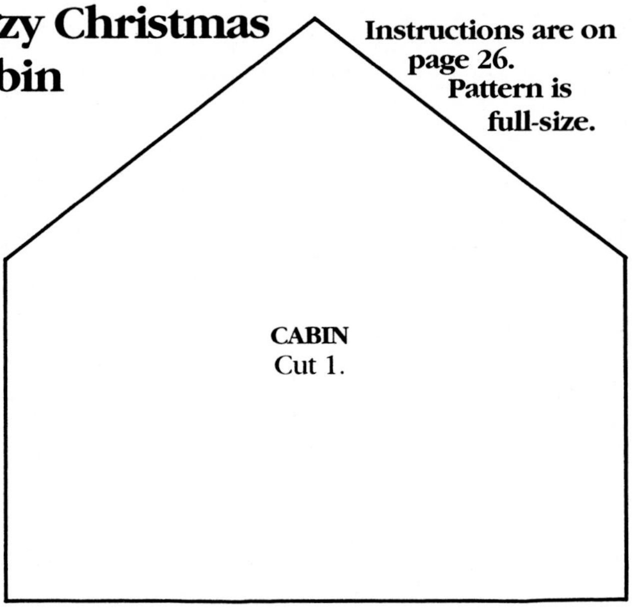

CABIN
Cut 1.

Snowflake Ornament
and Treetopper

**Instructions are on page 28.
Pattern is full-size for
ornament. For treetopper,
enlarge ornament pattern to
twice its size on copy machine.**

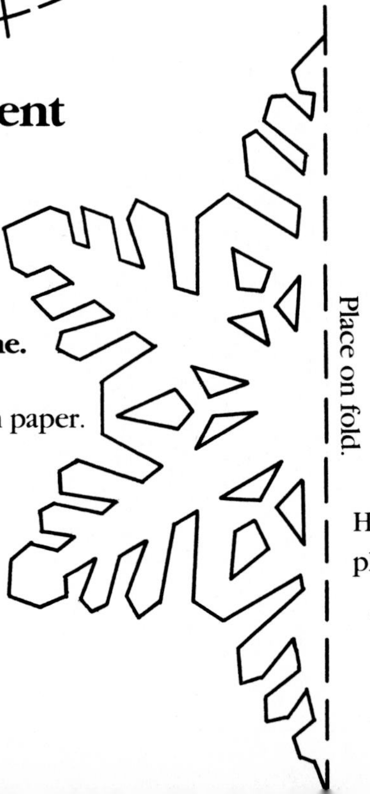

Cut 2 from cream paper.

Mittens-and-Snowflake Garland

**Instructions are on page 26.
Patterns are full-size.**

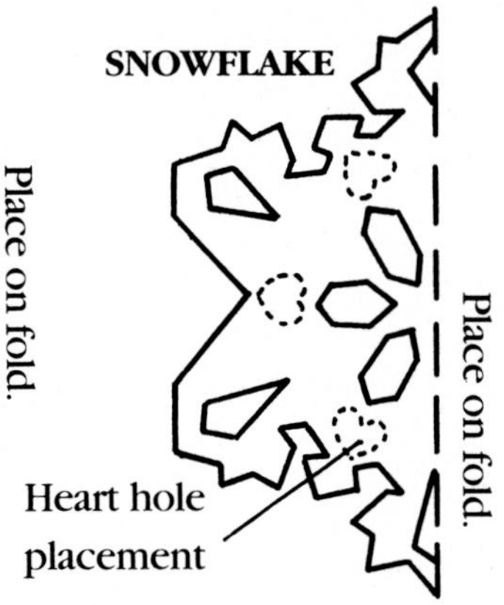

SNOWFLAKE

Place on fold.

Place on fold.

Place on fold.

MITTENS
Cut 8 pairs from
light brown paper.

Heart hole
placement

Hole placement

Cut 10 from cream paper.

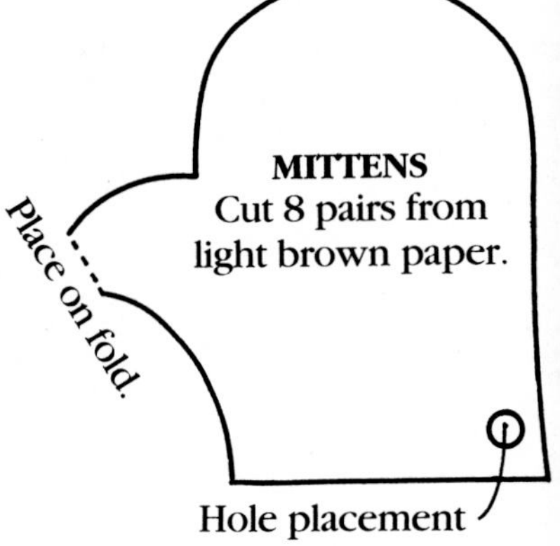

132

Reindeer at Night
Instructions are on page 29.

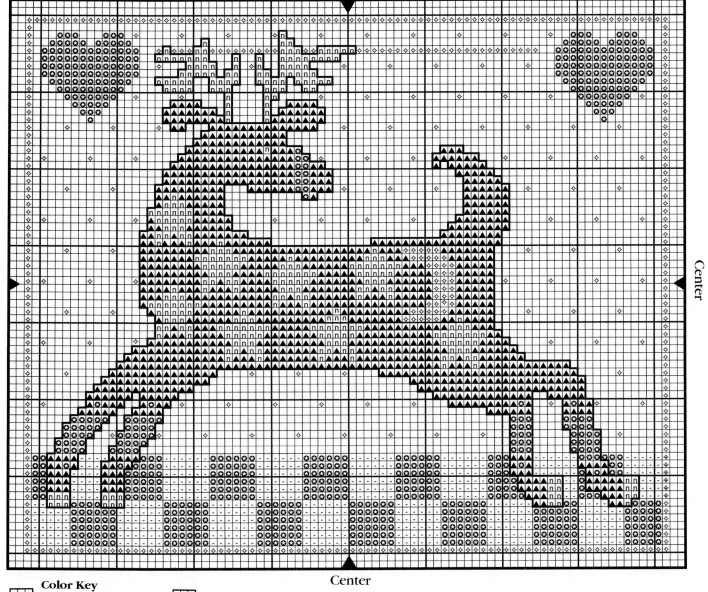

Center

Center

Color Key

−		White
▲	420	Dark Hazel Nut
◇	745	Light Yellow
n	809	Delft Blue
❀	3609	Light Plum

Note: Numbers are for DMC floss. Cross-stitch over 2 threads, using 2 strands of floss. Use 1 strand of 310 Black to backstitch reindeer and antlers.

Sculpt a Wire Wreath

**Instructions are on page 44.
Patterns are full-size.**

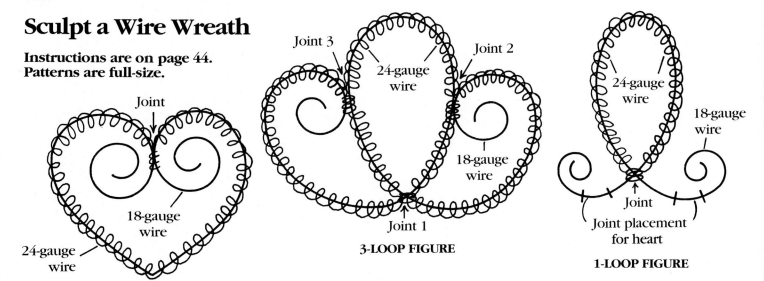

Joint

Joint 3
24-gauge wire
Joint 2

24-gauge wire

18-gauge wire

18-gauge wire

18-gauge wire

Joint

Joint 1

Joint placement for heart

24-gauge wire

HEART

3-LOOP FIGURE

1-LOOP FIGURE

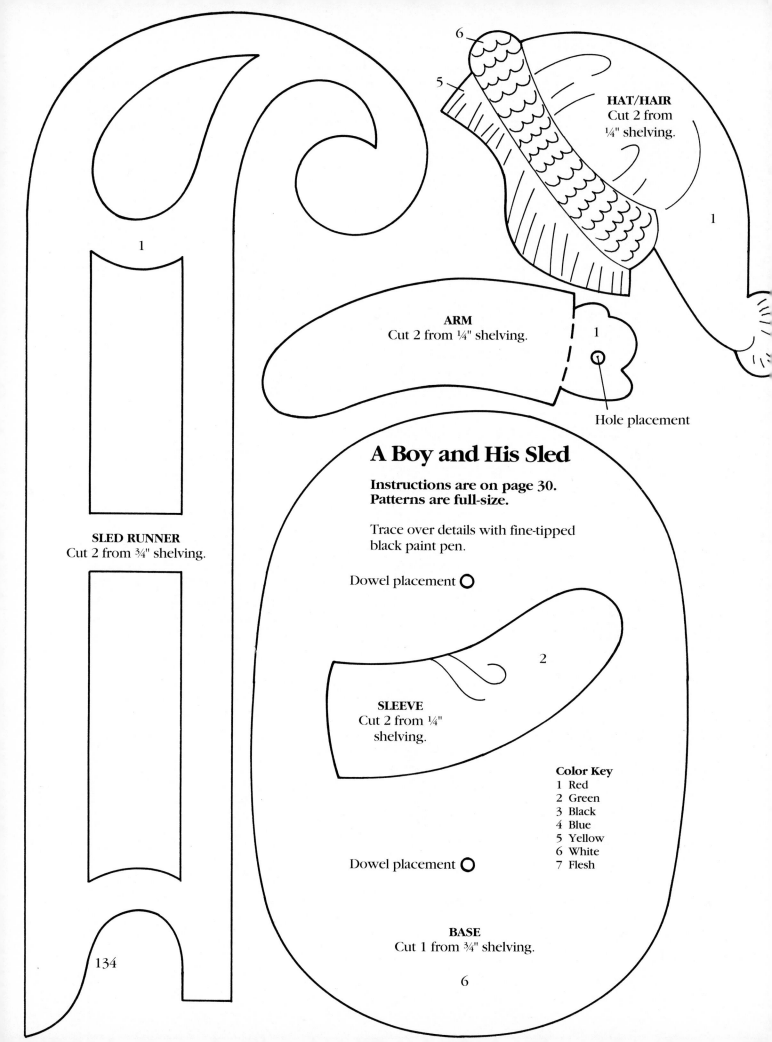

6

5

HAT/HAIR
Cut 2 from
¼" shelving.

1

1

SLED RUNNER
Cut 2 from ¾" shelving.

ARM
Cut 2 from ¼" shelving.

1

Hole placement

A Boy and His Sled

**Instructions are on page 30.
Patterns are full-size.**

Trace over details with fine-tipped
black paint pen.

Dowel placement ⭕

2

SLEEVE
Cut 2 from ¼"
shelving.

Color Key
1 Red
2 Green
3 Black
4 Blue
5 Yellow
6 White
7 Flesh

Dowel placement ⭕

134

BASE
Cut 1 from ¾" shelving.

6

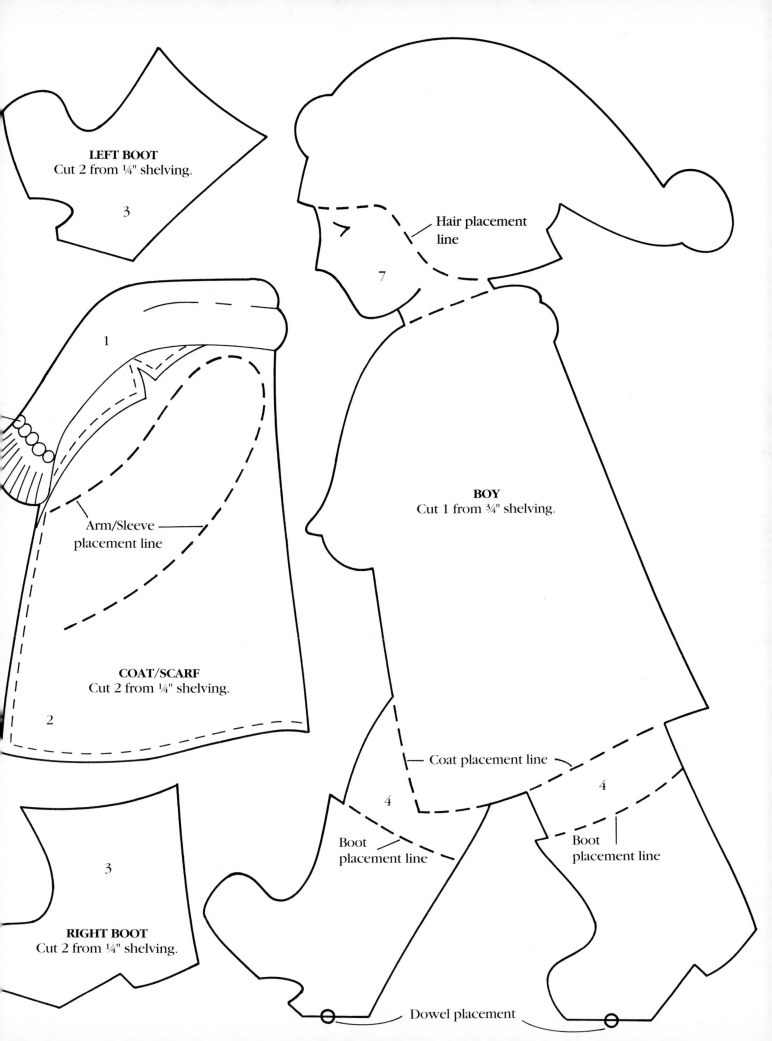

LEFT BOOT
Cut 2 from ¼" shelving.

3

Hair placement
line

7

1

Arm/Sleeve
placement line

BOY
Cut 1 from ¾" shelving.

COAT/SCARF
Cut 2 from ¼" shelving.

2

Coat placement line

4

4

3

Boot
placement line

Boot
placement line

RIGHT BOOT
Cut 2 from ¼" shelving.

Dowel placement

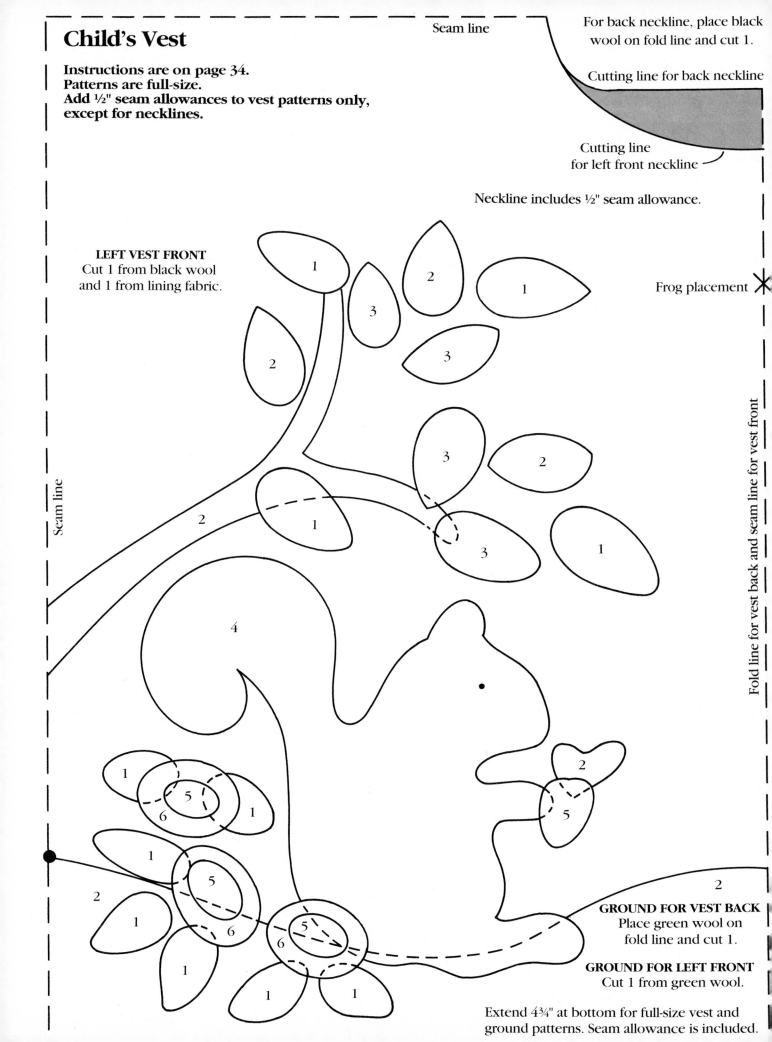

Child's Vest

**Instructions are on page 34.
Patterns are full-size.
Add ½" seam allowances to vest patterns only,
except for necklines.**

Seam line

For back neckline, place black
wool on fold line and cut 1.

Cutting line for back neckline

Cutting line
for left front neckline

Neckline includes ½" seam allowance.

LEFT VEST FRONT
Cut 1 from black wool
and 1 from lining fabric.

Frog placement

Seam line

Fold line for vest back and seam line for vest front

GROUND FOR VEST BACK
Place green wool on
fold line and cut 1.

GROUND FOR LEFT FRONT
Cut 1 from green wool.

Extend 4¾" at bottom for full-size vest and
ground patterns. Seam allowance is included.

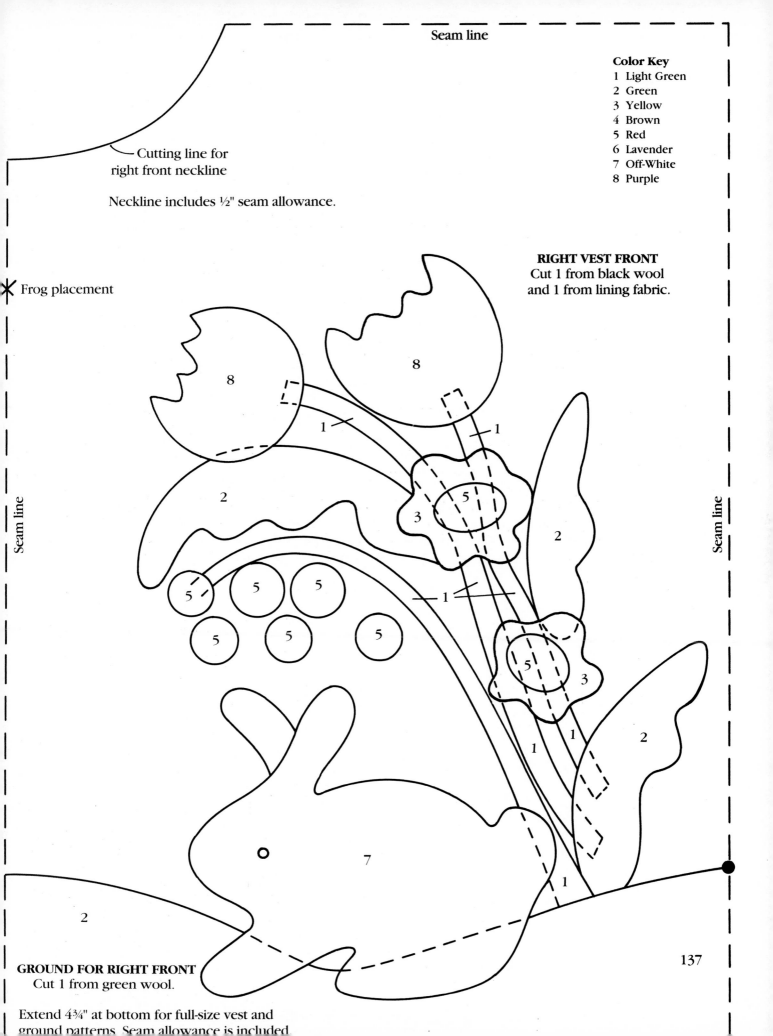

Seam line

Color Key
1 Light Green
2 Green
3 Yellow
4 Brown
5 Red
6 Lavender
7 Off-White
8 Purple

Cutting line for
right front neckline

Neckline includes ½" seam allowance.

Frog placement

RIGHT VEST FRONT
Cut 1 from black wool
and 1 from lining fabric.

Seam line

Seam line

137

GROUND FOR RIGHT FRONT
Cut 1 from green wool.

Extend 4¾" at bottom for full-size vest and
ground patterns. Seam allowance is included.

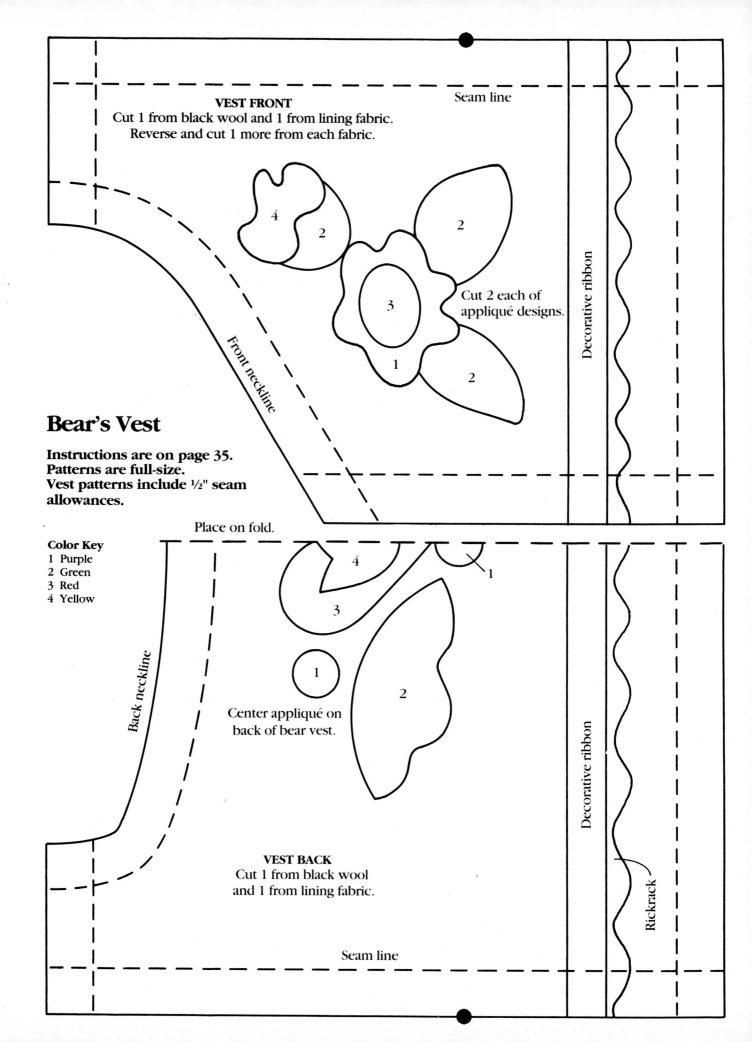

VEST FRONT
Cut 1 from black wool and 1 from lining fabric.
Reverse and cut 1 more from each fabric.

Seam line

Front neckline

Decorative ribbon

4

2

2

3

2

1

2

Cut 2 each of
appliqué designs.

Bear's Vest

Instructions are on page 35.
Patterns are full-size.
Vest patterns include ½" seam
allowances.

Place on fold.

Color Key
1 Purple
2 Green
3 Red
4 Yellow

Back neckline

4

1

3

1

2

Center appliqué on
back of bear vest.

VEST BACK
Cut 1 from black wool
and 1 from lining fabric.

Decorative ribbon

Rickrack

Seam line

Snowman Stocking

Instructions are on page 36.

Knitting Chart

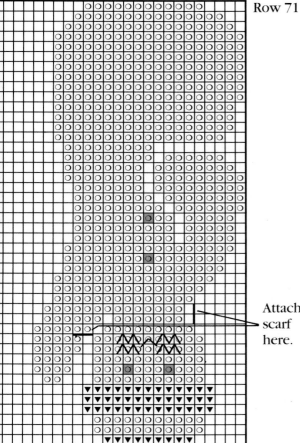

Row 71

Row 25

Attach scarf here.

Color Key

	Green
○	White
▼	Red

Tree-and-Snowflake Stocking

Instructions are on page 37.

Knitting Chart

Rnd 38

Rnd 10

Repeat

Note: To read chart, begin with Rnd 10 in lower right-hand corner and read back and forth across rows to top, rep indicated portion of design. Each row of chart represents 1 row of St st. Knitting Abbreviations are on page 153.

Color Key

*	Green
▼	Red
	White

Note: To read chart, begin with Row 25 in lower right-hand corner and read back and forth across rows to top. Each row of chart represents 1 row of St st. Duplicate-stitch cheeks with pink. Embroider mouth with red. With black, make French knots for eyes and buttons. Knitting Abbreviations are on page 153.

Feathered Friends

Instructions are on page 41.

Note: Numbers are for DMC floss. Cross-stitch, using 2 strands of floss. Use 2 strands of 444 Yellow to backstitch feet for cardinal and chickadee. Use 1 strand of 310 Black for remaining backstitching.

Chickadee

Blue Jay

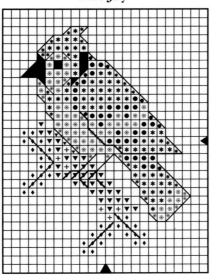

Cardinal

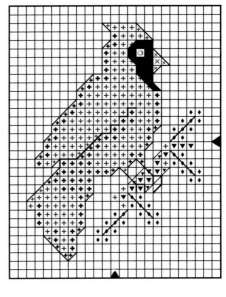

Color Key

+	666 Red		*	799 Blue		■	310 Black	I	762 Light Gray
	433 Brown		●	797 Dark Blue		▢	746 Cream		White
	700 Green		×	444 Yellow		▲	413 Dark Gray		
	800 Light Blue		+	498 Dark Red			318 Medium Gray		

139

Stenciled Hearts and Flowers

**Instructions begin on page 38.
Patterns are full-size.**

Note: Make stencils for ¼ of design, according to patterns. Refer to placement lines to stencil complete design. Broken lines are placement lines.

**DAISY STENCIL
ONE-FOURTH PATTERN**

**HEART STENCIL
ONE-FOURTH PATTERN**

Stencil patterns continued on next page.

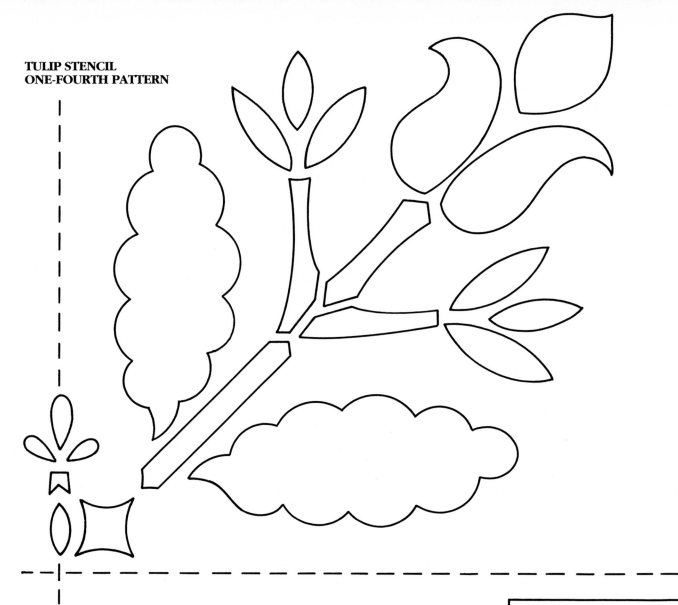

**TULIP STENCIL
ONE-FOURTH PATTERN**

Quick and Cozy
Winter Woolens

Instructions are on page 45.

Note: Duplicate-stitch designs,
using 4 strands of yarn.

Chart for Sweater Cuffs
and Neckline

Repeat

Chart for Mitten Cuffs

Repeat

Chart for Tree

Color Key

▼	Red
*	Green
×	Yellow

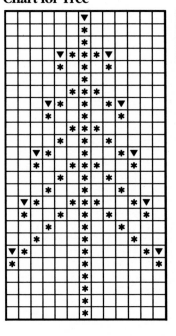

A Sprightly Trio

FACIAL FEATURES

142

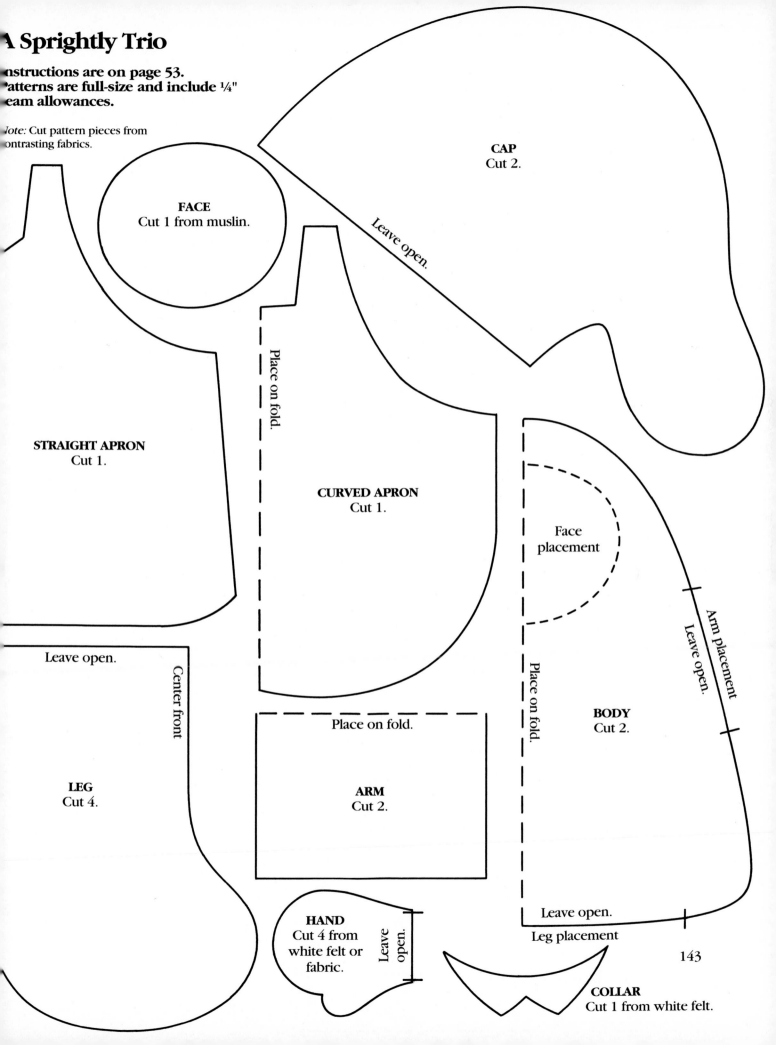

A Sprightly Trio

Instructions are on page 53.
Patterns are full-size and include ¼"
seam allowances.

Note: Cut pattern pieces from
contrasting fabrics.

CAP
Cut 2.

Leave open.

FACE
Cut 1 from muslin.

Place on fold.

STRAIGHT APRON
Cut 1.

CURVED APRON
Cut 1.

Face
placement

Arm placement

Leave open.

Leave open.

Center front

Place on fold.

BODY
Cut 2.

LEG
Cut 4.

Place on fold.

ARM
Cut 2.

Leave open.

Leg placement

143

HAND
Cut 4 from
white felt or
fabric.

Leave open.

COLLAR
Cut 1 from white felt.

A Prim and Proper Christmas Kitten

Instructions are on page 42.
Add ¼" seam allowances to all patterns.

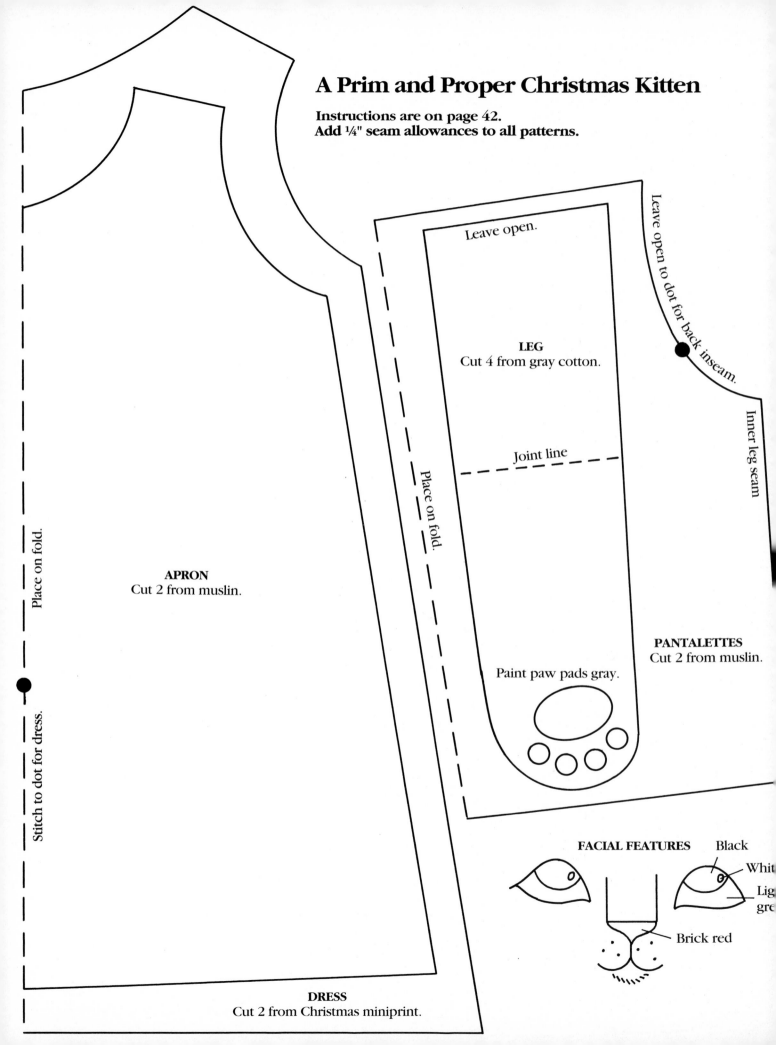

Leave open.

LEG
Cut 4 from gray cotton.

Leave open to dot for back inseam.

Inner leg seam

Place on fold.

Joint line

APRON
Cut 2 from muslin.

Place on fold.

Stitch to dot for dress.

PANTALETTES
Cut 2 from muslin.

Paint paw pads gray.

FACIAL FEATURES   Black

White

Light green

Brick red

DRESS
Cut 2 from Christmas miniprint.

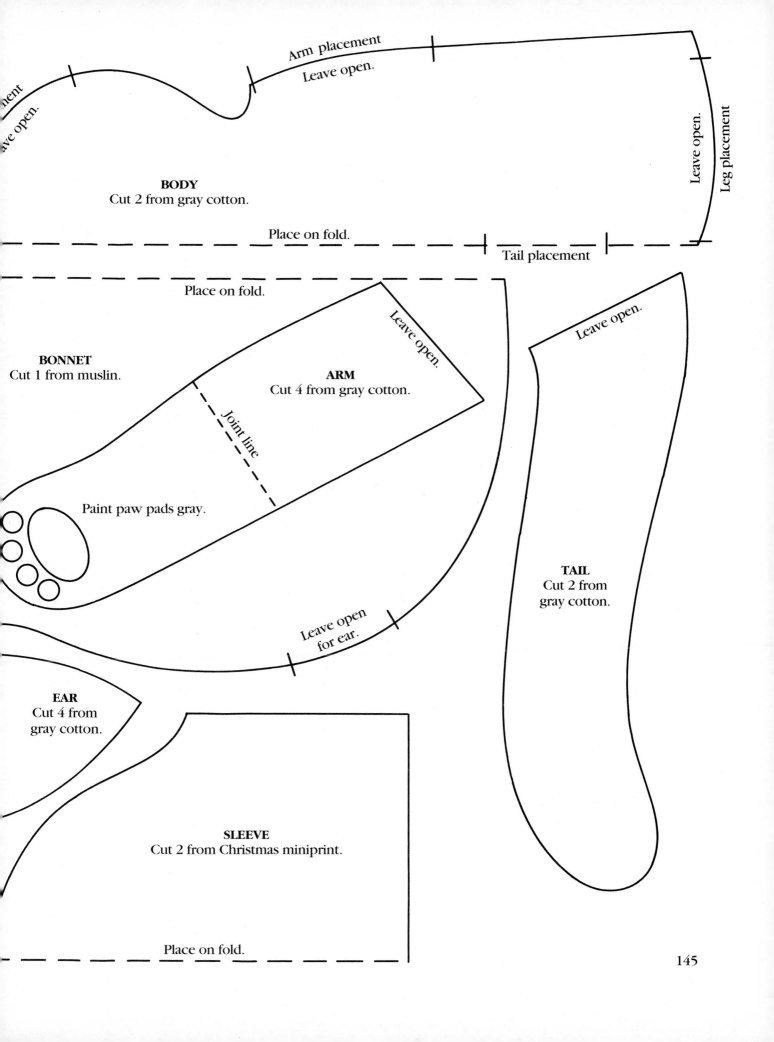

BODY
Cut 2 from gray cotton.

Arm placement
Leave open.

...nent
...ve open.

Leave open.

Leg placement

Place on fold.

Tail placement

Place on fold.

Leave open.

BONNET
Cut 1 from muslin.

Leave open.

ARM
Cut 4 from gray cotton.

Joint line

Paint paw pads gray.

Leave open.

TAIL
Cut 2 from
gray cotton.

Leave open
for ear.

EAR
Cut 4 from
gray cotton.

SLEEVE
Cut 2 from Christmas miniprint.

Place on fold.

145

Snowbound Stocking and Tree Skirt

**Instructions begin on page 48.
Appliqué patterns are full-size.
All patterns include ¼" seam
allowances.**

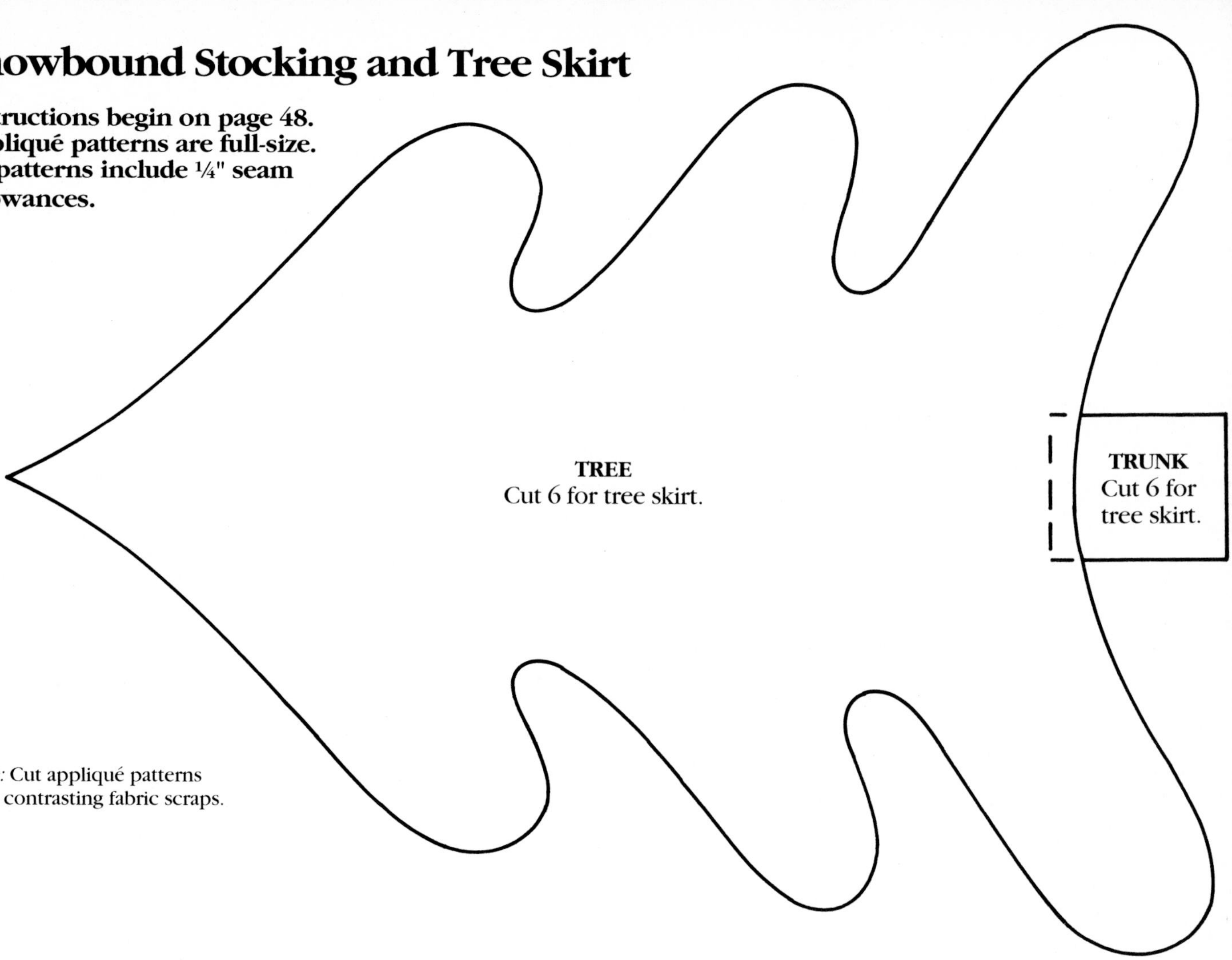

TREE
Cut 6 for tree skirt.

TRUNK
Cut 6 for
tree skirt.

Note: Cut appliqué patterns
from contrasting fabric scraps.

Each square equals 1".

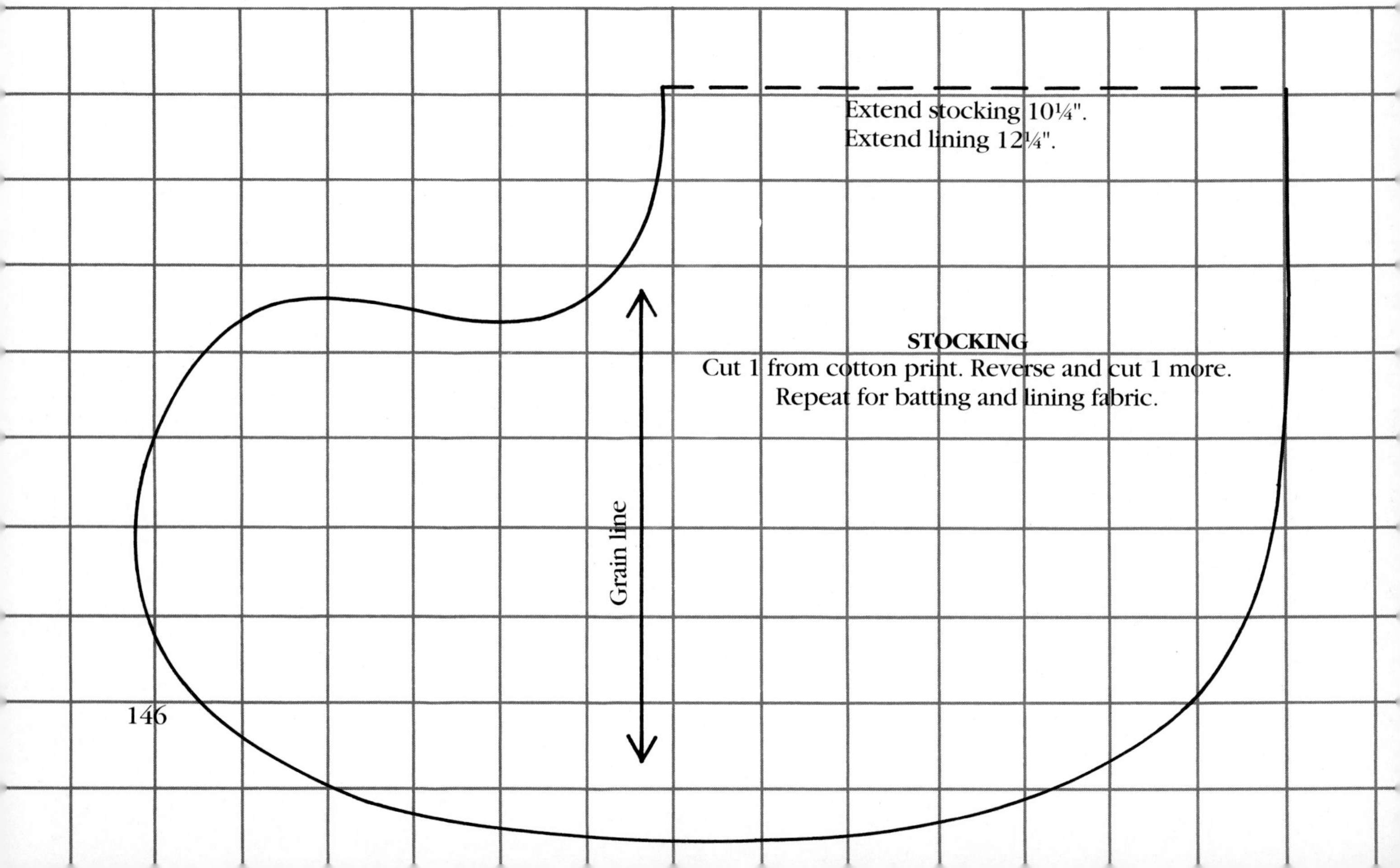

Extend stocking 10¼".
Extend lining 12¼".

STOCKING
Cut 1 from cotton print. Reverse and cut 1 more.
Repeat for batting and lining fabric.

Grain line

146

Each square equals 1".

STAR
Cut 3 for stocking.
Cut 1 for tree skirt.

TREE SKIRT DOG
Cut 2 for tree skirt.

Place on fold.

SNOWMAN TREE SKIRT PANEL
Cut 6 each for tree skirt top and backing.

Grain line

SNOWMAN TREE SKIRT
PLACEMENT DIAGRAM

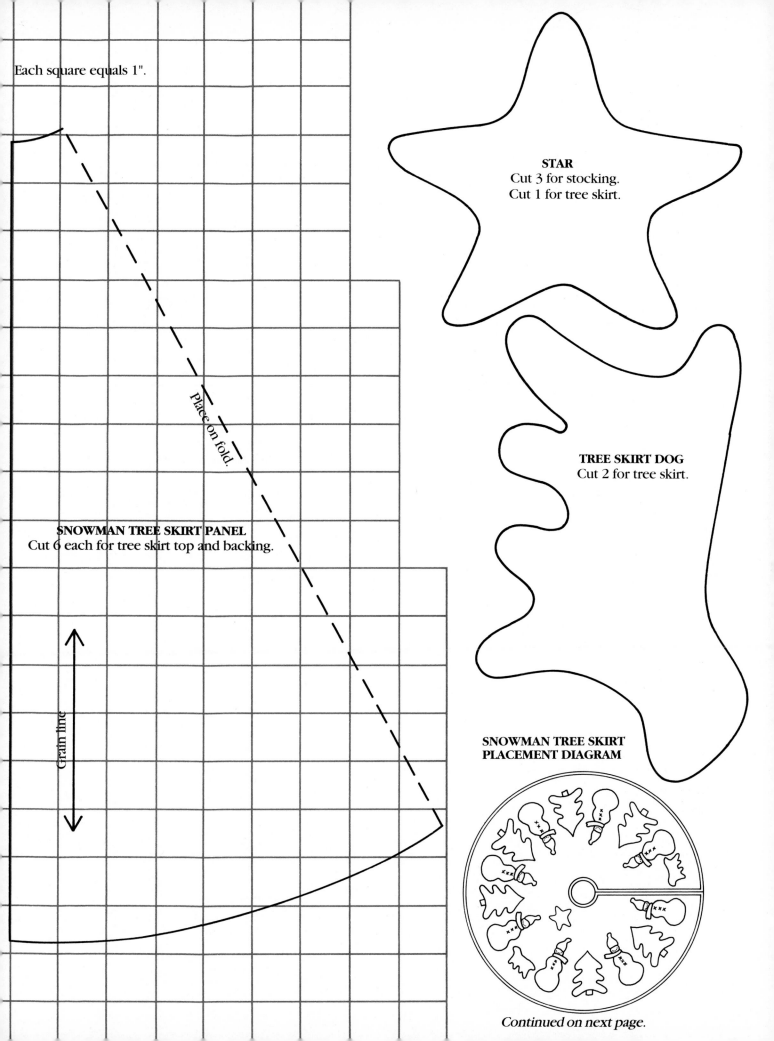

Continued on next page.

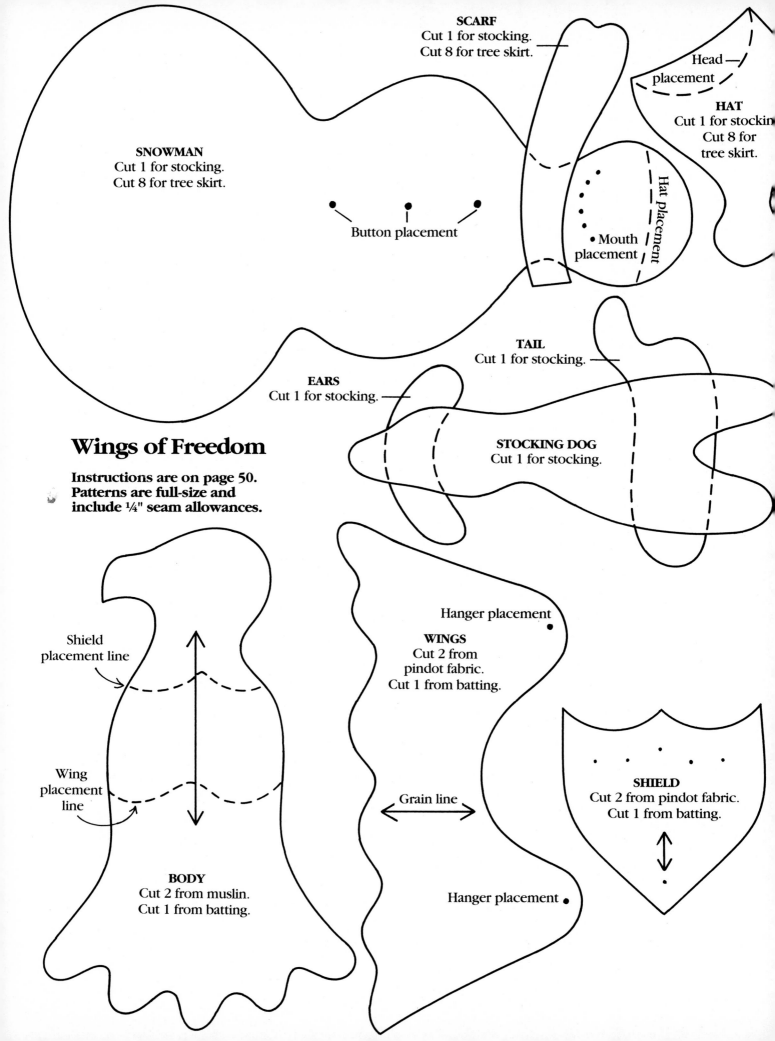

SCARF
Cut 1 for stocking.
Cut 8 for tree skirt.

Head —
placement

HAT
Cut 1 for stocking.
Cut 8 for tree skirt.

SNOWMAN
Cut 1 for stocking.
Cut 8 for tree skirt.

Button placement

Mouth placement

Hat placement

TAIL
Cut 1 for stocking.

EARS
Cut 1 for stocking.

STOCKING DOG
Cut 1 for stocking.

Wings of Freedom

**Instructions are on page 50.
Patterns are full-size and
include ¼" seam allowances.**

Shield
placement line

Wing
placement
line

Hanger placement

WINGS
Cut 2 from
pindot fabric.
Cut 1 from batting.

Grain line

SHIELD
Cut 2 from pindot fabric.
Cut 1 from batting.

BODY
Cut 2 from muslin.
Cut 1 from batting.

Hanger placement

Gleaming Ornaments

Diamond Ornament

Instructions are on page 64.
Pattern is full-size.

Hanger placement

Small tassel
placement

Small tassel
placement

Banded
tassel
placement

Amish Icicle

For instructions, see caption on page 63.
Pattern is full-size.

Cutting line

Moon and Star Ornament

Instructions are on page 64.
Pattern is full-size.

Hanger placement

Star placement

Bell placement

Embroidered Felt Ornament

Instructions are on page 64.
Pattern is full-size.

Cut 6.
Lay pattern parallel to stretchy grain of felt.

Grain line

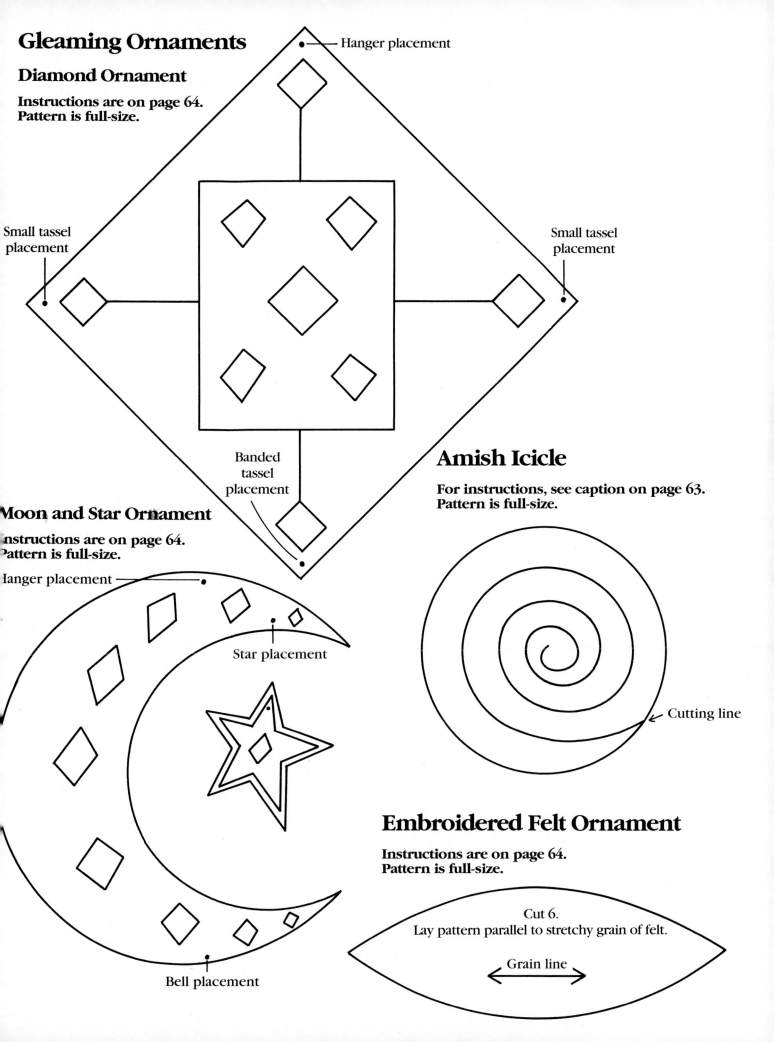

Framed Keepsake Reindeer

Instructions are on
page 73.
Pattern is full-size.

Cutting line

REINDEER

Decorative
Painted Jars

Instructions are on
page 99.

Refer to photograph for
color placement.

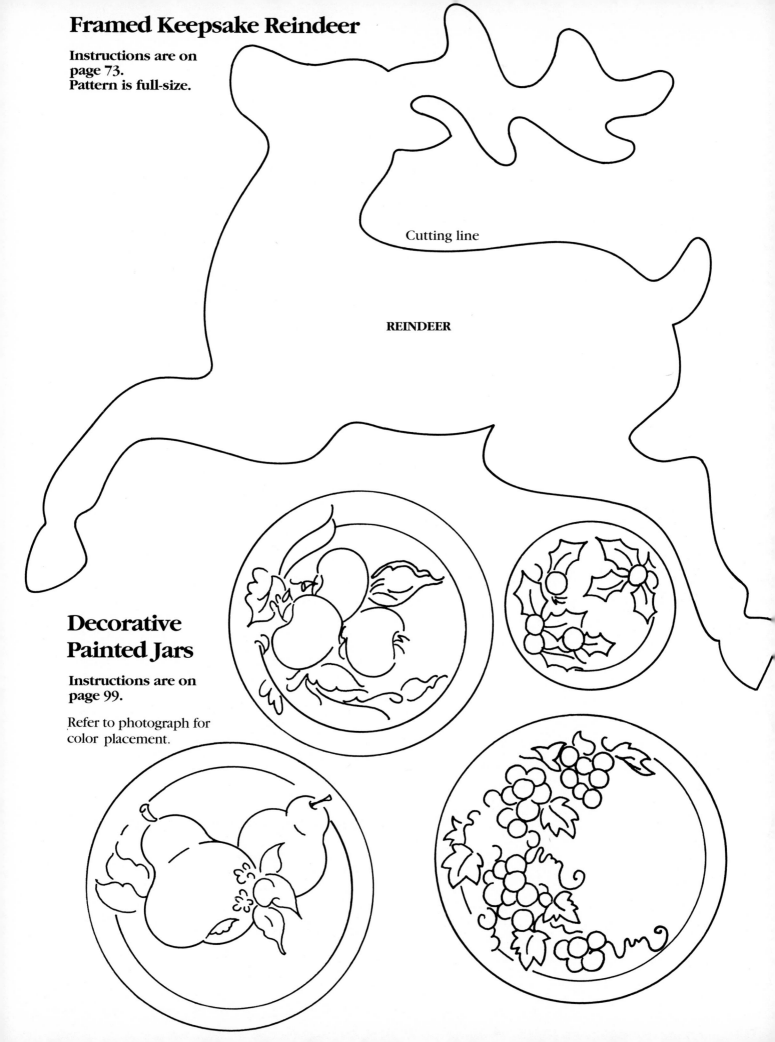

Woodburned Ivy Platter

Instructions are on page 89.
Pattern is full-size.

ONE-FOURTH PATTERN

Note: Make stencil for ¼ of border, according to pattern. Refer to placement lines to stencil complete border.

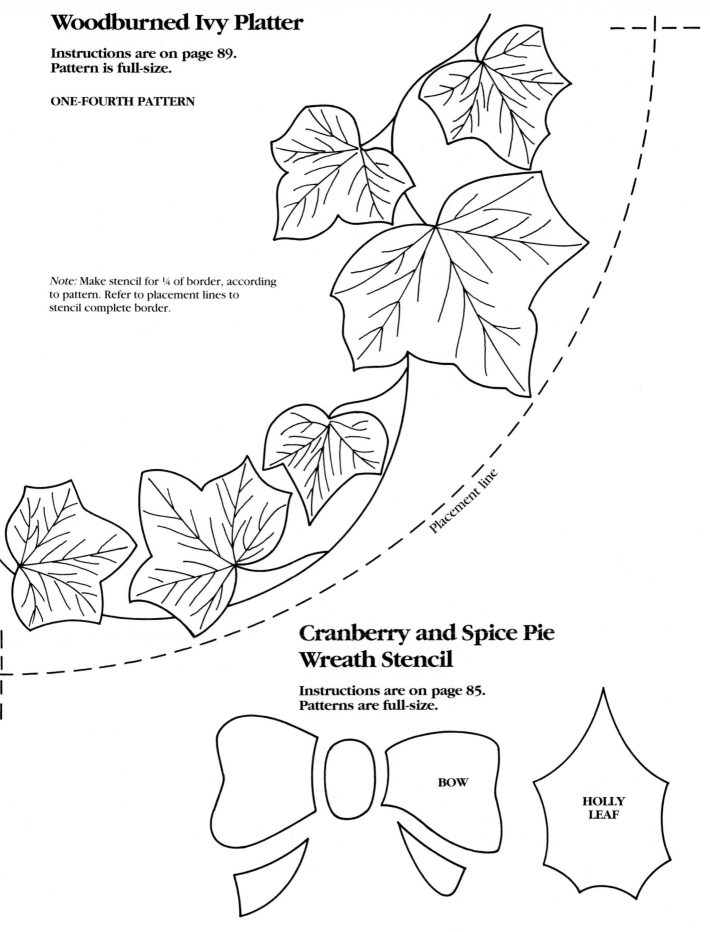

Placement line

Cranberry and Spice Pie Wreath Stencil

Instructions are on page 85.
Patterns are full-size.

BOW

HOLLY
LEAF

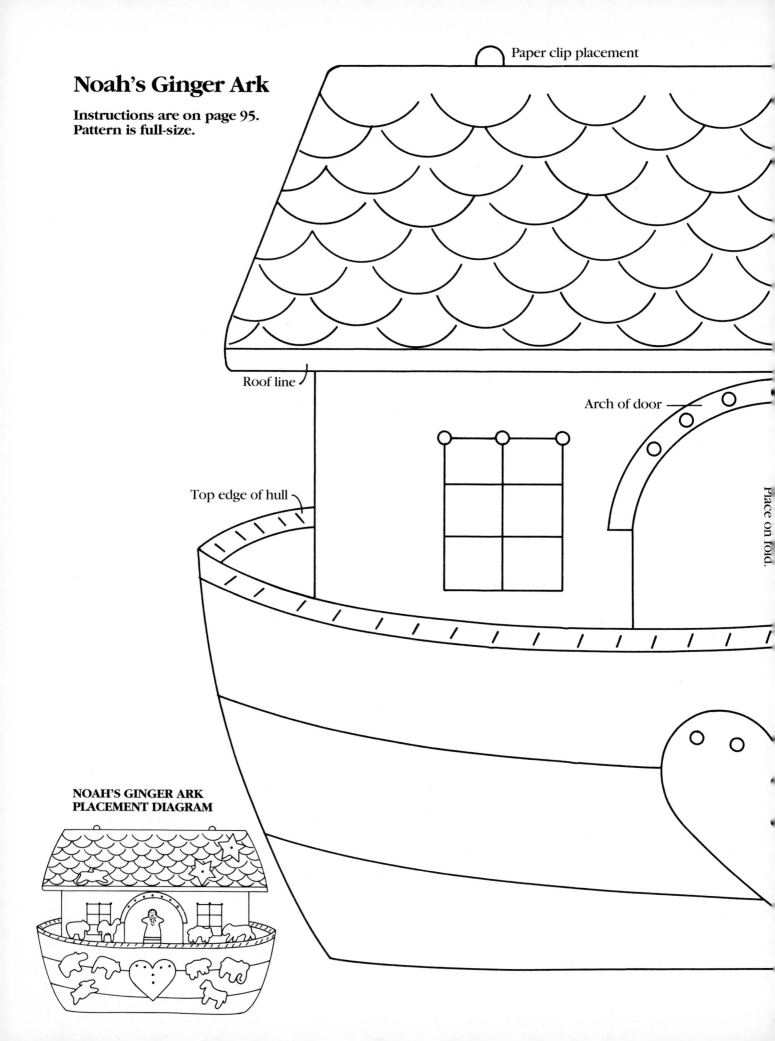

Noah's Ginger Ark

Instructions are on page 95.
Pattern is full-size.

Paper clip placement

Roof line

Arch of door

Top edge of hull

Place on fold.

**NOAH'S GINGER ARK
PLACEMENT DIAGRAM**

Cookie Cutter Ornaments

**Instructions are on page 110.
Patterns are full-size.**

Instructions are on page 110.

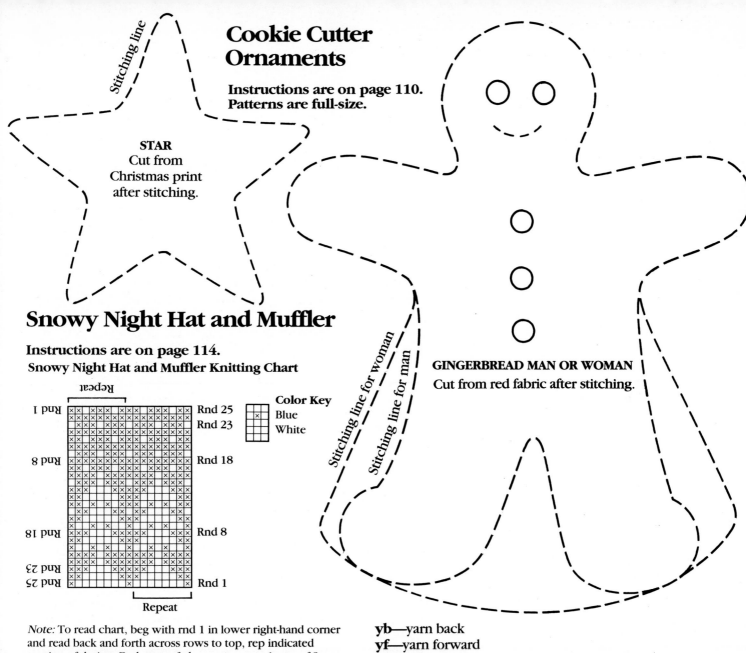

Stitching line

STAR
Cut from
Christmas print
after stitching.

GINGERBREAD MAN OR WOMAN
Cut from red fabric after stitching.

Stitching line for woman

Stitching line for man

Snowy Night Hat and Muffler

Instructions are on page 114.
Instructions are on page 114.
Snowy Night Hat and Muffler Knitting Chart

Repeat

Rnd 1
Rnd 8
Rnd 18
Rnd 23
Rnd 25

Rnd 25
Rnd 23
Rnd 18
Rnd 8
Rnd 1

Repeat

Color Key
× Blue
  White

Note: To read chart, beg with rnd 1 in lower right-hand corner and read back and forth across rows to top, rep indicated portion of design. Each row of chart represents 1 row of St st.

Knitting Abbreviations

beg—begin(ning)
dec—decreasing
est—established
k—knit
pat—pattern
p—purl
rem—remain(ing)
rep—repeat(ing)
rnd—round
sl—slip
ssk—slip, slip, knit (sl each st k-wise, k both sts tog through the back loops)
st(s)—stitch(es)
St st—stockinette stitch (k 1 row, p 1 row)
tog—together

yb—yarn back
yf—yarn forward
yo—yarn over
*****—repeat instructions following asterisk as indicated.
( )—repeat instructions in parentheses the number of times indicated.

Crochet Abbreviations

beg—beginning
ch—chain
dc—double crochet
lp(s)—loop(s)
rep—repeat
rnd(s)—round(s)
sc—single crochet
sl st—slip stitch
sp(s)—space(s)
*****—repeat instructions following asterisk as indicated.

153

Contributors

Designers

Carolyn Davis,
stitching on sweater and mittens, 45.
Susan Z. Douglas,
knitted stockings, 37; child's hat and muffler, 115.
Barb Griffin,
elves, 52.
Charlotte Hagood,
dried floral projects, 4-7; Victorian cornucopia, 6; rickrack candy canes, chenille icicles and stars, 27; design for duplicate stitch on sweater and mittens, 45; doll quilt, 60; crochet ornaments, embroidered ornaments, tassels, 63; tassel garland, 64; framed reindeer, 73.
Catherine Hoesterey,
cross-stitch reindeer, 29.
Pamela Houk,
yo-yo ornaments and garland, 119; yo-yo collars, 120.
Jellicle Original,
cat doll, 43.
Gerry Kimmel,
stocking, 48; tree skirt, 49.
Barbara Lavallet,
decorative jars, 96-97.
Charlotte Lyons,
paper fence, 21; child's and bear's vests, 35; Noah's ark cookie, 95.
Lelia Neil,
tassel earrings, 65; apple garland, 83; peppermint garland, 126-127; package topper, 127.
Carole Rodgers,
cross-stitch bird

wreaths, 41.
Katie Stoddard,
log cabin ornaments, 27; ivy platter, 89; barn wreath, 111; candy cottage, candy cane heart, 126; candy cane planter, 127.
Evelyn Thompson,
papier-mâché Santas, 54-55.
Carol M. Tipton,
tablerunner, 19; construction of log cabin ornaments, 27; mittens for garland, 28; boy with sled, 30; wire wreath, 44; vine doll bed, 60.
Joan Vibert,
eagle ornament, 50.
Sue von Jentzen,
mini-quilts, 27.
Carol Wagner,
door banner, 11.
Julie A. Wilson,
snowflake tablecover, 20; country borders, 21; paper jewelry, 56-57; Amish icicles, 63; moon and diamond ornaments, 63.
Cecily H. Zerega,
stenciled projects, 39-40.

Photographers

All photographs except for the following taken by **John O'Hagan.**
Ron Anderson, 74-75.
Gary Clark, upper right 4, lower right 6, lower left 21, 30, 39, 43, 51, 89, 95, 111.

Colleen Duffley, 52, lower right 77.
Mary-Gray Hunter, 73.
Hal Lott, 8-10, 70-72.
Beth Maynor, 12-15, 31-33.
Art Meripol, 19, lower right 21, 24, 28, 50, 55, 60, 63, 110.
Melissa Springer, 16-18, 112-113, 124-125.

Photostylists

All photographs except for the following styled by **Katie Stoddard.**
Gloria Gale, 74-75.
Susan Merrill, 67-68, 83, 87-88, 90, 93, 96-97, 99, 100, 104-105, 116-117, 121.
Joetta Moulden, 8-10, 70-72.

Sources

• Page 4-dried materials brochure: $1.00 to Meadowleaf Farm, RR 1, Box 290, Liberty, ME 04949-9707

• Page 18-Boat House Bed and Breakfast: 383 Porter St., Madison, GA 30650

• Page 26-*Scherenschnitte* supplies: Back Street Designs, P.O. Box 1213, Athens, AL 35611

• Page 47-Red Wagon books: Red Wagon, 439 Miller, Liberty, MO 64608

• Page 67-chestnuts: Chestnut Hill Orchards, 3300 Bee Cave Rd., Suite 650, Austin, TX 78746 or call 800-745-3279

• Page 72-Browning Plantation: Rte. 1, Box 8, Chappell Hill, TX 77426

• Page 75-Haderway House: P.O. Box 56, Lancaster, KS 66041

• Page 77-feather trees: Primitive Trees, Inc., P.O. Box 783, Cedarburg, WI 53012

• Page 78-filler pages/ photograph supplies catalog: Exposures, Inc., 9180 Le Saint Drive, Fairfield, OH 45014 or call 800-222-4947

• Page 126-candy canes: Bobs Candies, Inc., P.O. Box 3170, Albany, GA 31708

Special thanks to:

Earl Freedle
Margaret Allen Northen
Richard D. Tucker
Virginia A. Welch

Index

General

Recipes